STREET

TALK

STREET TALK

By: **Billy Wall**

Aim-Hi Books

1542 Lakeside Dr. West

Canyon Lake, Texas 78133

www.Aim-HiBooks.com

Aim-Hi Publishing
1542 Lakeside Dr. West
Canyon Lake, Texas 78133

Publisher's Catalog-in-Publication Data Names: Wall, Billy James, 1948 -; cover illustration: Russell Autrey _____

Title: Street Talk / by Billy Wall

Description: Aim-Hi Publishing LLC, 2022.
|Summary: Author's poetry based on various residential locations, and his memories of those places.
Subjects: Poetry | Memoir. | Bipolarism. | Newspaper Editing. | Impact of mental health conditions on relationships. | Treatment & Recovery. | Religion – Christianity. |Hope. |

Identifiers: Library of Congress Control Number:2022922443
ISBN 978-1-7374029-6-1 (Mass-Market Paperback)

First Edition: [December 2022]
Printed in the United States of America

9   8   7   6   5   4   3   2   1

STREET TALK

My Bipolar Struggle Street by Street

© 2022, Billy Wall

INTRODUCTION

This memoir chronicles my bipolar journey street-by-street. Each street drew me closer and closer to my bipolar disorder diagnosis.

Along the way, I developed a crushing case of obsessive-compulsive disorder.

I also started abusing alcohol.

Most of these mental issues came on gradually. And years before they were named.

These accounts span 73 years.

I wrote this memoir as a series of poems. I feel most comfortable in the poetic form.

My understanding of bipolar disorder is that it is a mental health condition that causes extreme mood

1

swings, including emotional highs – mania – and lows – depression.

I presented with the classic symptoms: In my depression, I felt sad and hopeless. From time to time, my mood shifted to mania, where I felt euphoric, full of energy, and unusually irritable. My mood swings affected my sleep, energy, activity, judgment, behavior, and ability to think clearly.

Oh, just so you know, there is hope. I eventually found it.

The street texts are long poems with short poems mixed in. I conclude with other selected poems.

1908 WEST HIGHWAY 21

About 60 years ago right there on the map of Bryan,
Texas
Is displayed 1908 West Highway 21
Where the action was
Some good, some sad, some spooky
Highway 21 is where I grew
From a one-year-old baby to a nine-year-old shy boy
And sometimes off and on
Throughout my teenage years
Mixed feelings abound in me
About my time on this three-acre plot
It was just inside the city limits
On a busy stretch of Highway 21
Only a few houses dotted the area
On the West side of town
Where the poor but proud and rugged folks dwelled
It was my dad's mother, Grandma Wall, who owned the
acreage
On it, about 50 feet from the highway,
Sat her house
Where my dad grew up,
Going to school, selling eggs, growing goats, and
working in the garden
The home was an old railroad building moved to the
property
Back in the first part of the Twentieth Century
Painted white, it sported a small front porch
It was proud and rugged too
A bedroom was added on some years later
My brother and I slept in the add-on
Some memories of Highway 21 are clear
Some are dim, if not completely vanished with time
I had a toy box I loved as a small child

3

It was wooden and on rollers
My dad made it
A letter carrier by career, he was also something of a
carpenter
I do not remember a particular toy in the box
Many were fuzzy and stuffed
One of my first childhood memories
Is of me peering into that box
Marveling at the abundance of toys
And taking one out
Just do not know which one
I lived there on Highway 21
With my grandmother, my dad, and brother
Until I was nine
My mother died in a car-train accident when I was one
My grandmother was my mother, for all I knew
Until I was six or seven
Then I knew
I do not remember grandma hugging me
But I am sure she did
She cooked and cooked scrumptiously
I think her love for us came through
In her cherry pies and biscuits and pinto beans
And her exquisite cornbread
Grandma was a tall, thin woman
With a constant bun made with her long hair
A bit of Indian blood coursed her veins
She was deliberate, matter-of-fact
It might be just me, but I do not recall her smiling
But I'm sure she did
I think her tough exterior formed with her sense of
responsibility
She saw two young boys
Who needed nurturing and disciplining
And her only child, my dad
Who craved normalcy for him and us boys

4

One vivid childhood memory
Is of me up a tree
Not just any tree but the sticky cedar tree out front
I knew I was forbidden to climb it
Never a rebel, I cannot figure yet why I did
"Get down from there right now!
This little stunt got to grandma
I do not recall her ever getting mad at me
Before or after
I got the switching of my life
It stung a little
But not much
It was not a brutal switching
Just a please-don't-do-that-again gentle grandma
whupping
It did the trick
The cedar oozed a glue-sticky substance anyway
This incident broke me from climbing all trees
I cannot say I missed it
I found other things to do
Like dig tiny foxholes for my toy soldiers
In an abandoned flower bed
Between the shiny tin garage
And an old unused chicken house
One year my brother and I got wagons for Christmas, I
think it was
Mine was smaller than his
With its bright wooden sideboards
Do not even remember what my wagon looked like
Just know I remember Arnold's for some reason
I think I liked it better than my little wagon
Arnold reminded me of the large vegetable garden
outback
He remembers hoeing and pulling weeds in the hot sun
He once found an Indian arrowhead among the rows
Cut his finger, daddy said

I keep a full-color snapshot of the garden in my mind
Grandma, Arnold, and dad worked in the garden in this
mental photo
Guess I was too young to work with them
But I cannot imagine not finding playtime there
That garden meant fresh beans and the like
In a time when such were at a premium
We lost Grandpa Wall to a heart attack
When I was still toddling around the house
Arnold was eight, which put me at going on five
As he lay dead on the couch in the living room
I peeked in and glimpsed him lying there, frozen
I did not understand
I just knew grandpa was not up and talking
I thought he was taking a nap
Except for the concerned faces of grandma and dad
I did not know him very well
My only remembering of him was when he paddled my
bottom
Because I wanted to go outside to play in the rare Texas
snow
Me looking longingly through the screen door
Seeing patches of white in the yard
It is the first time I recall wanting something, bad
Frustrated, Grandpa said, "You can't go out there"
He had to do more than coax
Grandpa's paddling was as soft as a kitten's paw
I did not even cry
But I did obey
Grandma or dad never talked of grandpa
I never asked
I wish I had
Arnold remembers one incident with grandpa
It involves Arnold's cracked head
Grandpa, driving my brother to school,
In his Model T Ford

Slammed on the brakes to avoid some traffic
No seatbelts, of course, Arnold smashed into the
windshield
The windshield cracked
But he was OK
Grandpa could heat up his fiddle with quick strokes
He loved to play
But I do not remember hearing his lively tunes
And he could sing
Arnold said all his siblings could sing
That trait missed me
 I realize now what grandma was going through back
then
Grieving her husband's death
Along with the weight of helping care
For two little grandsons
And her son grieving the loss of his wife
No wonder grandma's face seemed always somber
Grandma wanted me to care about God
She took me to a Pentecostal church when I was nine or
so
Hands waving in the air and shouts of "praise Jesus!"
Flew across the sanctuary
The congregants stood and began to sway
Hands still in the air
Came some "praise the Lords"
Preacher short, balding, and boisterous
Bible in one hand,
Pointing at us sinners with the other
I crawled under the pew
Or maybe not
The preacher said I might go to Hell if I do not get right
with God
I had heard of hell, that blast furnace down under
I figured I would end up there no matter what
There also was singing

That tempered the mood a bit for me
I just stayed close to grandma
I was not about to go up front during the call
Too scared even with the guilt I felt
I did not make up my mind about Jesus until much later
My dad remarried when I was nine
And we left Highway 21 for a while
Sometimes dad and my stepmom did not get along
Back to Highway 21, we went
My dad, my brother, and me
Meanwhile, the grass grew tall
On the front acre of Highway 21
My brother, three and a half years my senior
Drew the mowing straw first, being older and bigger
Arnold sweated and thirsted for a cool drink of water
While working a sputtering push mower
At some point, my turn came
I sputtered and sweated
Taming the stubborn Johnson grass
I had heard of riding lawnmowers
And dreamed of us getting one
An easy-mowing enthusiast,
I lobbied for a mower you ride
Way before they were cool
Meanwhile, I kept sweating and shoving
One day, somehow, someway
The brown beauty arrived
To my shock and awe
I could not believe it
I loved that riding mower
Though it was finicky
Sometimes hard to start
Not enough power for the front yard drop-offs
Anyway, there I rode in the Texas sun
Atop a roaring engine with blades
Trying for a tan and a mowed lawn

At 1908 West Highway 21
I often felt isolated
As I said, few houses nearby
No one nearby to play with
A big old three-acre lot
Almost out of town
No indoor toilet
The least adored part of town
I had to walk long distances to visit my school friends
Until I learned to ride a bike
I never felt quite at peace on Highway 21
Those were lonely times, but sometimes exhilarating
I rode my bike to visit Grandma Hall, my mother's
mother
Who was a Lanehart until she married Charlie Hall
When I was 10
I pedaled fast across Highway 21
Somehow failing to get flattened by a big truck
Uphill, my pedals got hard to crank
On the pot-marked side streets
On my way to 29th Street
I came to the intersection where I needed to turn onto
29th Street
For some reason, I whizzed past a stop sign
And into the path of an oncoming car
Car tires squealed at the sight of me
Frightened, I laid the bike onto the gravel
The elder couple got out of their car
"Are you alright?" the driver said, helping me up
I was, but I garnered some scrapes and bruises
I was a half block from Grandma Hall's house
Grandma Hall got me
And thanked the Lord I was all right
Shaken, I still had a good visit
Dad got me and my slightly injured bike
I never rode my bicycle to her house again

I learned to ride my first bike sans training wheels on
Highway 21
At first, my little silver bike sported training wheels
I remember the day the stabilizers came off
Training wheels went; dad steadied me
One hand on me and the other on the handlebars
He gave me a push and let go
I tumbled to the gravel
After dozens of tries, I finally wobbled off and away
Right into the side of the house
Bruising my sense of independence
My dad pushed me off one more time
I missed the house!
Oh, then there is the separate garage
A tin-clad affair
That looked modern
Compared to the house
My grandpa and dad built the garage
It had two sliding doors for two cars
My dad made it into a mini woodworking shop at one
time
Complete with a table saw, a plainer, and other tools
I was fascinated with this for sure
I itched to create something in wood
One day when I got a little older
I cranked up the table saw
Although I knew I should not
Not having any idea what I was doing
I put a piece of scrap wood on its table
I heard the whirring of the motor starting up
The blade whizzed in a furious circular pattern
I pulled the wood along
Pulling and pulling as the blade ate through the wood
Yes, I watched the wood too long
Instantly blood spewed from my right thumb
I snapped it back in time to save the digit

It left a small scar I can hardly see now
I never told anyone about my blunder
In my early teens, I had a magazine collection in the garage
I placed the magazines neatly between the exposed two-by-fours
I filled the walls with them
I nailed cross pieces to the studs and placed the magazines in the pocket it made
Eventually, they lined the walls
Provocative faces and figures looking longingly at me
My main motive?
Nothing sinister
The airbrushed pretty ladies, of course
This was the first sign of my obsessive-compulsive tendencies
That manifested big-time years later
Mesquite trees covered the back half of 1908 West Highway 21
A forest of five-foot scraggly things
Limbs bristling with one-inch thorns
Could not see past those trees to the back property line
We were forbidden to enter
Only one summer I defied grandma
This is one of the few transgressions I recall
That thicket held secrets, I was sure
There was a powerful pull to it
I must explore one day, I thought
One summer day I could not resist
I walked barefoot past the fence gate
Defying God and grandma
Bad move
I stepped once, twice
And then there were three
"Ouch," I said.
Yes, ouch

For I did not cuss
My grandmother never cussed around us boys
Never heard dad cuss either
Oh, that day I stepped on a mesquite thorn
I pulled it out of my heel and went limping to grandma
A little soaking in warm water and a bandage
And I survived
Neither grandma nor God scolded me
Both felt I learned my lesson
I had a terrible experience with a match
Way before the incident I am about to impart
I either burned my hand or came close to it
Ever since I feared matches
Now, here is why I mentioned that
It plays a bit part in the truth I'm about to tell
The summer before my sixth-grade year
A school friend came walking by our house
There Murry strolled on Highway 21
Cars and trucks whooshing by
I called out, "Where are you going?"
"To get some fireworks," Murry said
Murry soon was out of sight
As he marched toward a firework stand
Located just past the city limits
No fireworks sales were allowed within the city limits
I hardly knew Murry from school
So, I surprised myself when I called to him
I was more than shy most of the time
Murry, a stocky 11-year-old
Returned 30 minutes later
He popped through the gate of our chain-linked fence
Staggering under the assortment of
Firecrackers, cherry bombs, TNT bombs
And a few other exploding or whistling items
No sissy sparklers
My brother, not menaced by matches

Met Murry and they hatched an action plan
Yes, a simple plan it was:
Light the cherry bombs and TNT bombs
And toss them so they would blast midair
Timing was everything
With my match aversion and fear of the major
firepower
I decided to simply watch
Unafraid, Murry and Arnold tossed dozens
Of the powerful big boys
Booms split our ears
Powdery smoke hung in drifts
It smelled like gunpowder
Arnold and Murry soon began a ritual fraught with
danger
They would light one, rare back their arm
And wait
And wait
Then launch just in time
Getting a little heavy, they would say
As the fuses sizzled down to the bombs
The guys laughed and laughed
Until
Yes, there is an until
Murry reared back and waited
"Getting a little heavy," Murry fatefully said
Just then he flung the cherry bomb as usual
Boom!
Just inches away from Murry's hand
Blood followed the blast
Murry was stoic
Nary a tear
Turns out the explosion broke his thumb
I saw him later at school wearing a beige sling
Wonder what he said when the teacher asked
What did you do last summer?

13

Oh, we found out later Murry had stolen the fireworks
money
From his mother's change jar
I'm not sure grandma knew what was going on
She was stunned
Anyway, many lessons learned
I do not do fireworks now
Except at a far distance
Arnold?
"Getting a little heavy," I think I heard him say recently
He said, "It could have been me"
Let me tell you another story
An only-on-Highway 21 story
One night dad and I lounged in the living room
Watching some black and white TV show
Only a screen door between us and the whizzing traffic
Everything normal
A little boring
That ended when we started hearing a strange sound out
in the dark
Above the roar of highway traffic came
Something like a coyote howl
It was whisper-close
But it was no whisper
Frightening at first, until dad spotted the source of the
howls
Dad called me to come out to view the cause of the eerie
sound
It was car tires spinning desperately at high speed
The car attached to the racing tires lay straddle our
driveway culvert
Wheels hanging off both sides
The driver sat semi-slumped in the driver's seat
Gunning the engine in a rush to get his white sedan to go
forward
The sound?

The rubbing of tires spinning on gravel
We assured the heavyset balding driver he needed help
"Shirtenly, I do not!" the middle-aged fellow said.
After a little drunken monologue, the driver tumbled
out
Slamming the door on his fingers, hard
Some of his drinking buddies arrived to take him home
A tow truck eventually arrived to free the man's abused
car
See, what dad called a beer joint rested a block over
Facing Highway 21
Cars weaving away from it were commonplace
But this was a new one, dad said, as we both had a belly
laugh
We had a dog once, for an instant
The stray showed up one day
And we took it in
His name I cannot recall
A chow mix, long tan fur
A day or so later, a big truck ran over it
I did not see it happen
My dad broke the news to me
Did not get a chance to love it, or care for it
We never had a dog thereafter
One day a kid across the highway came over
To show off his new BB gun
Long and shiny with a hair-trigger
I stood in front of the boy and the gun
Pop!
He accidentally shot me in my thumb
It left a BB-sized indention
I was cautious around guns ever since
Once living on Highway 21
My dad took me deer hunting in a state forest nearby
It was shivering cold at dawn
I climbed into a tree with my rifle

15

Dad shimmied up a tree nearby
I did shiver and peered into the woods for a long while
We saw no deer, but it is a good memory
Never deer hunted again
I might need to tell you about my dairy days
The summer before my senior year in high school
I got a job offer I will never forget
It was to work on a dairy owned by the parents
Of Woody, a fellow on the school track team I was on
He was to go work on water drilling rigs
And I was to take his place on the dairy
Each day grandma made sure I was awake at 3 a.m.
I drove my 1956 Ford along in the dark
Some 45 minutes to the dairy barn
Then the same drive in the evening for the second
milking
Heavy-laden cows needing milking
Bursting with the urgent need of relieving their udders
Of their fresh white liquid
Moved to milk stations
Where I gingerly slipped on a milking sleeve on each
teat
"Be careful you do it right," Woody said
Do it wrong, and the udders develop a terrible condition
Besides milking, I shoveled manure
Lots of manure
I was fascinated with the dairy process
Woody showed me the large metal storage container for
the milk
Located in an air-conditioned room
Well, that job lasted a whopping two weeks
Woody said I could take my leave
Disappointed?
Relieved I was
Woody had graduated before that summer
I have not seen him since

Grandma's days on this earth ended
When I was a senior in high school
She lay peacefully in her bed when Arnold found her
At home
On 1908 West Highway 21
Those three acres looked different last time I went by
The house?
Sold and moved to another location in town
Weeds were tall and thick
My brother and I are not there to mow them
The garage?
Torn down
Mesquites still reigned on the back half
Although fewer
Memories?
Some good, some sad
That formative time at 1908 West Highway 21 proved
necessary for me
I developed a work ethic I still maintain
It provided a loving family atmosphere
Sadly, I found a bit of OCD there although I did not
know it at the time
And depression which also rose full-blown down the line
Yet I did have happy moments
Learning to ride bicycles
Playing in the dirt with my army men
Running track at high school
Overall, I say bless grandma and that three-acre plot
They help form who I am today.

126 WAVERLY DRIVE

This street was home to me off and on for many years
It is where an 825-square-foot bungalow still stands in
Bryan, Texas
My first actual memories of the house came well after I
was born
If my infant one-year-old little eyes could talk to me
They would tell of my first year of life
A life then lived at 126 Waverly Drive
My first encounter with the location
I wish my younger eyes could show my older eyes
tender hugs and kisses
From my mother, who died when I was one year old
I have a colorized picture of her pretty face
Lips parted in a smile, lovely brown eyes, looking
happy
Sometimes think of what I missed
Perhaps this
Lying in my wooden crib and crying. Amanda, my
momma says,
"Hush little Billy, don't you cry"
Tenderly, she plucks me up, holds me skin-close, and
says,
"You're wet, little child
Let us get you a dry diaper."
Momma lovingly lays me down, unpins the soaking
cloth diaper
Washes and dries me, and applies something powdery to
my baby bottom
Then deftly adds the new diaper.
I whimper again. Momma says,
"Are you hungry? Let's fix that"
Up I go again into momma's warm, soft arms
And I take in the milk I crave

Halfway through, momma says,
"You need to burb, baby boy"
Over her heaven-to-touch shoulder, I go.
I soon utter a familiar air-releasing sound from my baby mouth
Momma says, "There you are"
I finish feeding, and momma says,
"Time for a nap, little one"
Momma settles into a rocking chair
Holding me to her bosom, and slowly, gently rocks
Soon, I am in that sweet state of dreaming,
Of mom and dad and big brother, Arnold
Or my favorite blanket
Momma, with the stealth of a deer, rises and puts me back to bed
Momma says, peering down at her precious one
"Sleep well, my little prince"
Momma tiptoes out, her house shoes making soft footfalls
The above account I hope is more than dreaming
I must have heard my momma's voice back then
Of course, I do not remember it
A sweet soprano voice full of life and love, I am sure
I think I hear her now: momma says, in her tender voice
"Love you to the moon and stars, little Billy"
I never got to call her momma
Later, I never called my stepmother momma
The word did not seem quite right on her
I missed MY momma, although she was a mystery to me
I did come to love my stepmother
Even later, when my three young sons called their mother momma
I smiled inside

I am so happy they had, and still have, a loving momma
I am grateful my sons found beautiful and wise wives
Who make the most precious mommas to their sons and daughters
We lived there on Waverly – my father, my mother, my older brother, Arnold, and me
I remember nothing of that time, but I want to think we were a happy little family
After my mother died, dad and we boys moved back in with my Grandma Wall
To 1908 West Highway 21, which was larger than Waverly
Dad rented out 126 Waverly for many years after that
I moved back in some 18 years later
When I entered nearby Texas A&M University as a first-year student
I lived alone on Waverly for a couple of years
As I pursued my degree in journalism
During that time, my dad, a letter carrier, dropped in for a visit sometimes after he finished work
The post office was direct across the street from the house
We would talk there in the living room of 126 Waverly
He in his postal uniform and me in my college grunge attire
Office scuttlebutt was his usual topic
A regular postal soap opera that was fascinating to me
Dad knew how to tell a story with humorous detail
"George is going to quit (the post office) to go to another job
He got in a pickle with his wife
Got caught with a woman half his age who works at a laundry
Guess he got his comeuppance
'cause his wife is going to take him to the cleaners"

20

A hardy laugh blasts forth from his tanned face after the
punchline
Sometimes he talked about troubles with post office
management
He hated getting shadowed on his route by an inspector
Other times he spoke in hushed tones about my
stepmother
They did not always get along, and I would hear his side
I never heard my stepmother's side
Did not want to
I was not on good terms with her myself at the time
Then he would go to his home on Brazos Street across
town
Where he lived grudgingly with my stepmother
"She wouldn't give me a divorce," he said once
In his later years, Dad forgave, and they stayed together
until his death
Two years later, I fell in love
It was my junior year at A&M
More on that in just a minute
I never dated in high school
I hardly had guy friends, let alone girlfriends
Shy till it hurts shy and afraid I was diseased
A feeling I felt for years without proof
But I dated a couple of girls once I started college
One girl, I dated several times and felt close to her but
not in love
She was tallish, thin, with long brown hair and a
pleasing face
The second girl I dated was much too young for me
After two or three dates, I decided to move on
She did accompany me to a high school track meet in
Waco, Texas
I felt loyal to my Bryan Broncos track team
I ran track for the Broncos all through high school
Nothing happened romantically on that trip

Sex scared me
Was I going to give someone an imagined disease?
What about babies?
I ghosted the two girls, and I still regret it
I feel I should have found the courage
For a face-to-face
This still gnaws at me when I think of those days
I left the last girl after a fateful introduction to another
girl
A high school friend of mine and his girlfriend
A classmate of the mystery girl
Set up a meeting
I showered, shaved, and shook
I'm not clever at dating, I told myself
Will she run away when I say hello?
We all met somewhere I do not recall
Would she be pretty?
Smart?
Crazy enough to date me?
At the introduction, I was struck silly
Before me sat a pretty, smart
High school senior two years younger than me
We bonded over months of dating
We never did anything wild
Just dinners and trips to a nearby lake
Then I proposed
I do not remember exactly how
But I'm sure it was romantic
My first wife and I married in 1969
In a small Baptist church
The night before the wedding I got worried about my
bangs
Too long, I thought
Snip, snip, snip
Bad mistake
Our wedding pictures prove it

My bangs resembled a mouth with the front teeth missing
I sat in the barber chair ever since until my wife Debbie began trimming my locks
We made 126 Waverly Drive our first home
I found life there wonderfully peaceful and loving
Soon we took on a grey toy poodle named Amy
I remember as if it were yesterday seeing Amy's little trail in the snow
In our front yard after a rare Bryan snowfall
I also remember Kent, our firstborn
Dressed in his little winter coat, heading out to play
"Shoes on," Kent would say if he was ready to play
One time while visiting the LBJ presidential library in Austin
Kent spotted a scruffy-looking college kid visiting the library
"Dirty shoes," Kent said, pointing to the shoes
We were mortified
Did the college kid hear?
We rushed our tour
Many beautiful memories were formed on Waverly during this time
In 1971, something big happened when living on Waverly
My first of three boys, Kent, was born
Life in the two-bedroom house changed
For the good!
Baby bottles and formula and rocking baby to sleep became routine
Kent was a true joy
We were so proud of this little guy, who grew up to be a great father himself
Kent enjoyed Waverly
Toys in every room
And a shower of smiles from this tike

Oh yes, I graduated from Texas A&M in 1971
Kent's birth outshined that achievement
While living on Waverly and going to A&M
I went to work for the hometown newspaper, The
Eagle
Taking complaints in the Circulation Department part-
time
The Eagle is where I went on to work for 30 years
In my first days at The Eagle, I saw something blazed in
my memory
A linotype click-clacking away in the composing room
A single operator sat at its keyboard
The stub of a cigar attached to his tightened lips
Of this thin, rugged baseball-capped gentleman
A haze of cigar smoke partly vciled the sight of the
awesome machine
It rose some six feet from floor to top
A maize of moving metal parts
As the man pounded the keys, lead dropped into the
appropriate place
Forming lines of type
Lines dropped into the columns of a form fit metal tray
When full, the tray held the start of a newspaper page
I will not get into the particulars of how it all works
Enough to say it fascinated me as a 19-year-old budding
journalist
That linotype soon was packed on a train and railed to
Mexico
Along with the outdated giant press
Making way for a fancy, new offset press
Oh, the linotype was replaced by electronic typesetting
machines
By the time Kent was born, I was a reporter
On the day of Kent's birth,
My boss sent me to cover something away from the
office

Soon I got THE call
To Bryan Hospital I rushed
In time to pace a bit
A brief time later, the doctor told me we had a boy
It seemed like an enormity of time before I saw him
A nurse brought him to show me
The bottoms of his little feet were blue
I about panicked until the nurse assured me it was just ink from taking his footprints
Kent was a boy, but I still thought him beautiful
My wife made it through the birth fine
Later, we all three headed back to 126 Waverly Drive
While on Waverly, my wife and I got hooked on the soap opera All My Children
There we would sit, as they say, glued to the TV
As murder, mayhem, and romance danced on the small screen
We followed the regulars and the new ones cleverly introduced
A character would lie in a coma for weeks, barely-there
A character rose from the dead at least every other year
I crafted a feature article for the paper on our love of the show
Unfortunately, I do not have a copy of the article
One event I remember sadly involved our 1966 light blue Mustang
I was driving
My wife sat in the passenger bucket seat
This was before Kent
We rode along on a neighborhood street
Going the speed limit, I promise
Seatbelts seat belted, I promise
Out of the corner of my eyes, I saw it coming on the driver's side
Crunch!
A car roared through the intersection without looking

Crashed into the poor little unassuming Mustang
Crinkling the front fender
My wife hit the dashboard, which raised a lump on her head
I survived without as much as a bruise or a scratch
The other driver, from out of town, justifiably got the ticket
That injured Mustang was my wife's first car
Given to her by her parents for graduation from high school
My heart sank at the thought of her car now sitting idly in the garage
But I do not know what else I could have done
My wife's injury healed quickly
I was depressed during all this time
I felt scared as a parent and a man with a high-pressure job
I did not know how to be a father
And I worked and studied all the time it seemed
I was too busy for Jesus
We lived in Waverly for several months before feeling we needed a bigger house
A house of our own
We bought one on 24th Street, leaving 126 Waverly Drive for good
Arnold and I inherited the house when my father died, and we eventually sold it
I'm retired to Florida now and have not been back to Waverly in years
Google maps show the house still standing some 50 years later
It is almost the way we left it
Still painted white with a small porch at the front door
I painted the exterior at least twice
One difference is the front yard is highly landscaped
And the street is getting gentrified and "apartmentified"

With a new five-bedroom house for sale on the other end
of Waverly
And apartments beckon renters
I am proud of 126 Waverly Drive
It housed me when I was a baby
And when I was in college
And when I was married
Even now, it provides a quaint home environment for
someone
So, here's to you 126 Waverly Drive
May you live on for another seventy-five years.

BRAZOS STREET

In my second life journey,
My dad, my older brother, and I moved to Brazos Street
in Bryan, Texas
That is where I came of age
That is where I felt like I finally had a real family
One that included a mother -- my stepmother Jenny
Dad remarried for the first time since my birth mother
died in 1947
It was 1956
I was nine and my brother, Arnold, was twelve
It was before the marriage that I knew my mother had
died
It saddened Arnold and me that we had no living mother
Even though I loved my Grandma Wall, my father's
mother,
Whose house Dad and us brothers lived in with
grandma
On an isolated three-acre lot on the far western edge of
Bryan
Grandma's house was an ancient no-frills abode
Oh, running water but no indoor toilet
Yes, we did our business in an outhouse during the day
Slop jars in the house at night
I say all this to give you an idea
Of how fortunate we felt to be moving to Brazos Street
An indoor toilet!
And a real neighborhood with close neighbors
The Brazos Street house was the longtime house of
Jenny Little
And her kids Don, Judy, and twins Nelda and Neal.
My later years made me realize the gravity of that family
dynamic

My dad took on four small stepchildren
And Mom took on two young boys and their father
Dad was a mail carrier, Mom was an elementary school
secretary
Soon it was certain that the three-bedroom wood frame
house
Needed a larger bedroom for the four boys
And a second bathroom, one just for us guys
The girls had their bedroom in the front of the house
This new home came with a backyard and adjacent
vacant lot
Perfectly made for us boys as well as the neighborhood
boys
My early days on Brazos Street were spent in that
backyard
A small yard by grownup standards,
It was quite big enough for games of spinning tops
Draw a circle on the ground,
Place everyone's top in the ring
And take turns with your top
Knocking someone else's top out of the ring
I was not particularly good at it
Neal and Jimmy Nowak from the corner of our block
And Jerry Maxwell, who visited his nearby uncle on
occasion,
As well as Arnold was better than me at the game
Of course, they were two or three years older
Games of tackle football filled the vacant lot
With several neighborhood kids
Older than me and rougher than me
They let me play occasionally
But my body was small and the big kids
Did not want me playing
I sometimes tried to join the big boys
In a blockwide Chinaberry fight
Until slingshots were added

Slingshots raised stinging welts to the body
I remember once playing tackle football
In our small front yard
A lush layer of St. Augustine grass carpeted the ground
Taking some of the stings out of being wrestled to the turf
Neal, always a fierce competitor, tackled me hard once
But my belt buckle, forged into the shape of a cowboy boot
Caught him and drew blood
That ended that evening's game, which was lit by the porchlight
I remember Gary, the only kid in the neighborhood my age
We played in the backyard sometimes
Then there was that tunnel
Yes, we dug out a hole in the dirt floor of his grandmother's shed
Big enough for both of us to fit in is how I remember it
We were proud of our work
But his grandparents were not
You see, Gary only occasionally stayed with them
There in the comfortable house behind ours
His granny and grandpa were sweet people
And now I understand their frustration
That was the only time on Brazos Street I got in trouble
It was good that Gary was not there too often
Oh, the trouble he would have gotten us into
On my own, I was quiet and retiring
Unlike today when I am
Well, quiet and retiring
It took me a while to get used to having close neighbors
Back then, I was the definition of "shy"
Always looking for approval and love
I got love and approval from the whole family
And the whole neighborhood

I felt comfortable and safe
Mom was pretty and short and straight in stature
I received many a loving hug from her
Oh, could she cook!
Her dinner rolls rivaled gourmet cooks' attempts
Golden brown and scrumptiously moist
I have not found their match yet
Christmas time brought out her best cuisine
I mean peanut brittle that works your teeth and your taste
buds
Fudge, dark and rich
Snow white divinity, light on the tongue
Cakes and cookies and pies galore
I used to sneak the peanut brittle
Mom knew, but she never said anything
A moist turkey and all the fixings topped things off
Along with those famous yeast dinner rolls
We all devoured our meals in the dining room
A room I still recall as formal
Yet all eight of us clanking our forks and knives
And chattering made it most informal
Christmas also brought decorations
And special napkins for the table
The Christmas tree, always fresh
Put off a sweet aroma
Dozens of gift boxes lay beneath the shining tree
When nine, my present was exactly what I wanted
A bright red football helmet
Complete with a grey nose guard
Now, Don, the oldest of the kids,
Seemed more like a grownup to me
He once bought what I thought was a marvelous,
magical machine
A stereo
I liked Don's good taste and love of all things electronic
I would get home from school

31

And there alone in the house I did the unthinkable
I took a Johnny Mathis album out of its jacket
Placed it on the turntable and as precisely as I could
Set the needle on the vinyl
And heard Johnny croon out "Chances Are"
I never told Don about it
But I bet he knew because even I detected scratches on
the record
Due to my imprecision
I was the baby of the family
I was the smallest, ugliest, and dumbest of the family
I figured I proved the dumb part one school year
I was horrible at math
So, I would sit at the kitchen table
Trying to do my math homework
While the rest of the kids watched The Untouchables
Starring Robert Stack in the next room
I never improved on my math skills
One reason I later took up journalism
But that is another story
I remember playing cards on Brazos Street
With Nelda, Neal, Don, Judy, and Arnold
I hardly knew what cards were back then
We played Spades and sometimes Hearts
MY heart was happy when playing cards with my
brothers and sisters
Even though my card skills were shaky at best
We had some mean Monopoly games as well
Just before Hurricane Carla hit Galveston on Sept. 11,
1961
My mom's sister and two teenage sons
Came up from Galveston to Brazos Street to dodge the
storm's wrath
As a 13-year-old, I felt a little strange with the company
Everyone got along and over a few days
I grew accustomed to the visitors

Thankfully, Carla did no damage to the sister's home
While on Brazos Street, I played Little League
With my dad as the coach
I moved around from right field to pitcher a couple of times
I do not remember striking anybody out or catching a flyball
I played basketball in the ninth grade,
Following my brother, who had a stellar basketball career in high school
My basketball career was not so stellar
In the ninth grade, I did make a layup at a tournament in Huntsville, Texas
Peck Vass, the high school basketball coach, was in the stands
I impressed him apparently
Unbeknownst to me,
I was enrolled in the jock PE class when I started the tenth grade
I tried out for basketball right away
That was the end of my basketball career
I switched to track and ran the half-mile the rest of high school
My insides transformed into a hormone-raging teenager on Brazos Street
I felt alone in my change
Not realizing every teen goes through it
My urges were overpowering, but I never even went with a girl
I never talked to anyone about my plight
I did relieve my urges, alone
And felt the guiltiest of guilty and embarrassed
During those days, the Nowaks, who lived on the corner
Were good friends with my new Brazos Street family
August, the father, took me to Bowie Elementary School one year

We bounced along in his ancient sedan
I mean it had running boards it was so old even back
then
After dropping me off, he headed to his banking job in
town
August, a tall, thin, and balding dad
Talked little, but when he did it came in quick bursts
His son, Jimmy, played with us occasionally
I still remember the hum of our whole-house water fan
And the cool and moist and sweet-smelling air it blew
out
The huge contraption hung in a window in the den,
where a couch and chairs beckoned
I can still see my dad lounging there reading Newsweek
Magazine
As he basked in the cool, watery air
I got my first car on Brazos Street
A 1956 black and white Ford sedan
With a Thunderbird engine
It was some seven years old at that time
So, the fancy engine sputtered more than it sparked
It required weekly quarts of oil
Once when I was a teenager, the doorbell chimed
And Gary stood before me
I had not seen him in years
All grown up, I failed to recognize him
Until he said he was Gary from my early days on Brazos
Street
He is the Gary who used to visit his grandmother, who
lived behind us
Gary and I played together
It took me a bit before I remembered
He did not remind me of the fateful tunnel we dug
Perhaps he did not remember
For some reason, I was distant
He noticed and left quickly

I felt I just could not relate to this guy from my past
My journalism conviction began on Brazos Street
It was the ninth grade
Dad and my stepmother visited my English class
During open house
My teacher told them I have a writing gift
She pointed out the story I wrote in class
Where I described a galloping horse with flowing mane
My parents seemed impressed
Later, in high school, I was enrolled in the journalism class
Where Mrs. Edwards changed my life
She encouraged me no end
Named sports editor of the school newspaper, the Lariat
I explored writing for publication
It included interviewing fellow students who played basketball, ran track, etc.
Then I wrote news stories from those interviews
My column, named From the Wall, I thought looked good in print
All this learning primed me
For nearby Texas A&M University's journalism program
I eventually graduated and had a 30-year newspaper career
When I was an older teen, things got dicey between mom and dad
Arnold, Dad, and I bounced from Brazos Street
To my Grandma Wall's house where I had lived until I was nine
I never really knew all the details of the troubles
I suspect Arnold and I were in there somewhere
It was my senior year in high school
We had had enough of the moving
And headed sans dad to Grandma Wall's in 1966

The year of my high school graduation
Grandma Wall died at home that same year
I never lived on Brazos again
Years went by before I drove by the Brazos Street house
Dad moved back into Brazos Street and lived out his days there
My stepmother remarried after my dad's death and moved out
The last time I went by, the house looked a little drab
The white exterior faded
The front yard was not as green and seemed a lot smaller
I guess I mowed the grass some, although I do not remember it
My time on Brazos Street brings bittersweet memories
I still love Don, Judy, Nelda, Neal, and Arnold
Although they all outgrew the house and left Bryan
That is, all but Nelda, who still lives in the city
My stepmother lived into her late nineties right there in Bryan
To end this, I say happy trails to us all
As we continue to move beyond Brazos Street
Rest in peace dad and my stepmom
I'm sure they both went to heaven.

24TH STREET

In the early '70s, my first wife and I bought a regal home
On 24th Street in an ancient part of Bryan, Texas
It was just a few blocks away from The Eagle
The newspaper where I eventually worked for 30 years
It was the three of us
My wife, me, and my first son, Kent
We financed the home through a bank
I recall sitting in Dick Hervey's office asking for the mortgage
I was a young reporter, in my early 20s with deep brown hair
My wife was a young woman in her early 20s with long dark hair
I mention my hair because it soon turned salt and pepper, then all salt
Anyway, Dick, a former mayor
And then the president of the bank
Knew how to make us feel important when he said
"Yes, you are a fine young couple; I will be glad to make this loan"
The home was a beautiful, tall piece of art to us
With 12-foot ceilings, and part of the attic built out into a bedroom
Constructed around 1923 by a former mayor of Bryan,
The home sported asbestos shingle siding
Which I always wanted to tear off
And expose the original wood clapboards
Never did, just too expensive and too much work
And now I know it was dangerous too
So, the exterior stayed white shingles
But we added our touch: yellow trim

37

I bought a 36-foot aluminum extension ladder
Wrestled it to its full 36 feet and placed it at the front gable
There I inched up to nearly the top wrung
With a paintbrush and paint bucket in one hand
The ladder in the other
I tentatively started to paint the historic wood trim
I never felt safe balancing there in the clouds of 24th Street
Up at least 30 feet at the peak
Trying not to look down
Did get it all done eventually
The house consisted of a large living room,
Two bedrooms, a bathroom, and a half all on the main floor
And the one bedroom upstairs
I gained some repair person creds on 24th Street
I painted the outside trim
And I did the impossible in the kitchen
I installed a ceiling fan
That required a three-foot conduit
To bring the paddle fan down to the proper level
To this day, I do not know how I did it
They call it dumb luck
I wonder if it is still there
Kent took the attic bedroom
A new arrival -- my son, Mark
Rested in a crib in the second bedroom
When I said Mark rested, I laughed to myself
See, Mark hardly slept at night
He would not cry
We would find him simply standing in the crib and looking around
Oh, Mark would sleep during the day
I remember a horrifying moment with Mark on 24th Street

My wife and I bathed Mark in the bathtub often
One day, I plucked Mark out of the tub and stood him on
the side of it
Still wet, we were about to dry him off when I let him
slip for a second
Mark bumped his chin on the side of the tub, and blood
spewed out
At first, we could not figure out why he was bleeding
from the chin
The side of the tub was smooth and rounded
Instantly, it did not matter
We rushed him to the hospital
It took three stitches to fix up his little chin
I can still see Mark lying there
With the doctor adding the stitches
I felt faint
I remember Kent enjoying his upstairs room
Cardinals used to crash into his bedroom window
My wife stayed home with the kids
And she remained ultra-busy with them
I rode my bike to work for a long time
Which meant I seldom drove the used pickup truck
A truck I bought from my father-in-law
Who was selling to get another pickup
It was a fine Chevy truck, though ten years old
Brown with a small eight-cylinder engine
OK, I always thought it was a grandpa truck
I laugh now, for I AM a grandpa
I grew sad when I finally sold it
It would be a classic now
We would walk to a neighborhood park with the kids
Where they cavorted on the slides and swings
And on the empty baseball-field dirt
Home again, we quickly bathed them
My father-in-law, George, wanted me to learn to love
fishing

We decided
The next day in the predawn dark
I rose and pulled on my jeans, T-shirt
And what I hoped were fishing shoes
George arrived in his pickup at the predetermined time
We were to do some trotline fishing in the nearby
Navasota River
A complete novice, I listened with some nervousness
As George assured me trot fishing was fun and fulfilling
We were to check the trotlines already floating away
The evening before George set out six trotlines
And baited them
George taught me that trotlines are long fishing lines
With hooks dangling from the lines at set intervals
The lines are tossed into the river
A float on the end keeps the lines from dragging the
bottom
Catfish
That was the goal
I helped George check the lines
Pulling each hook up one at a time
Caught catfish wriggled and flopped on every hook
George grew ecstatic at the haul
He put them on a stringer
We dashed home to 24th Street and knocked on our back
door
Still early, my wife answered in astonishment
As I raised the stringer for her to see
Did George hook me on fishing?
You can tell from my unsure description of the sport
I chose the never again approach
Wish I had a do-over on that
I loved George and with a different attitude I could have
made it fun
When my dad died, I inherited a German Shephard
named Elsa

40

She was huge and a bit rough around the boys
We also had a tiny backyard
Also, Elsa reminded me too much of my dad's fate
He hung himself at his home on Brazos Street
So, we gave Elsa to someone who owned a farm
I regret that now, but it seemed best at the time
Dad, a quiet man, grew even quieter over the weeks
before his death
A heart condition meant he had to take medical
retirement from the Post Office
Where he worked for 30 years
Still in his 50s, he became despondent
No hobbies save for reading news magazines
He never found another job
And the idleness magnified his plight
A week or so before he died
He unsuccessfully tried to hang himself
The next day we sat at dinner at his home on Brazos
Street
Dad sat across the table from me
Bruises marked his sad face as he slumped toward his
food
I do not think he ate anything that night
In my late 20s, I tell myself I had not lived enough
To know how to talk to him
Dad never went to counseling
Oh, how I ache for going back
With the knowledge, I have now
Just days after that gathering
I got a call at the paper from my stepmother
Telling me Dad hung himself
I got to Brazos Street just before the paramedics
"He's in the pantry," my stepmother said
Should I rush in and cut him down?
I panicked and just sat on the couch
Small doses of adrenaline caused me to shake

My mind raced
What to do?
In an instant, the paramedics arrived
I still feel guilty that I did not jump into action at that time
Dad's death was not a total surprise due to his earlier attempt
I did not cry in public
But for several days I lay in bed in the dark
Sobbing off and on
This experience contributed to my depression, I'm sure
Although I couldn't at the time name the down feeling I had
That lump in my throat
That tightness in my chest
My wife, my kids, and my work kept me going
When Kent started school, we walked him the block over
I am still amazed at how brave Kent was in all things
We moved to 2311 Kent Street across town before Mark started school
Oh yes, Mark was a brave young man as well
We once hosted an Eagle newsroom party at 24th Street
That big living room was full of my workmates
I could not believe how many showed up
The banter was brisk and fun
I felt in the right place and loved and respected during that party
I have not been back to the 24th Street house in years
But I know how I remember it
A beautiful neighborhood punctuated by our beautiful house
White siding with light yellow trim
A large front porch

Well, one thing I know is not still there in the front yard
Is my yaupon holly I planted
I could not get it to grow
My neighbor, who was a coworker, said
"Nobody can kill a yaupon!"
But I did
And I never did grow much of a green thumb
I did grow many a beautiful memory on 24th Street
Yet a time laced with a tragedy that still haunts me
I would like to go back to the stately house one day
To see if my ceiling fan still blows breezes
To marvel at the height of the ceilings
To hear echoes of our early life
I will not come empty-handed
I will bring my shovel and some gloves
See, I will bring a fresh yaupon holly to plant.

2311 KENT STREET

In this section of my life,
There was the good, the bad, and the extremely ugly
I will get to the bad and the ugly after the following
On 2311 Kent Street in Bryan, Texas, I had all of it
Life was far from dull though
Tumultuous might be a better word
What with three boys growing up there
Before Kent Street, we lived across town on 24th
Street
With two small boys and a third one on the way
And a tiny, unfenced backyard
We needed more room and a playable yard
A more child-friendly neighborhood
2311 Kent Street was what we needed at the time
Our sons, Kent, and Mark, and our newest, David, filled
the new house
I was news editor at The Eagle newspaper by then
My first wife practically raised the kids by herself during
those early years
And if I am honest, most of their growing up
She worked with them all day long in the preschool
years
And put them to bed at night
I worked nights putting the paper to bed instead of the
boys
I should have gotten a day job
But I was doing well at The Eagle with lots of
responsibilities
And a team of coworkers working under me
Those daily deadlines put a lot of pressure on me
I oversaw the A Section
Which included the front page

The midnight deadline always seemed to come too
soon
I was consumed with getting everything right
Headlines that sing, stories properly edited
The whole section devoid of errors
2311 Kent Street consisted of three bedrooms
A small living room, a nice kitchen, a laundry room
And a small room we used as an office
The three bedrooms worked for awhile
But Kent and Mark were getting crowded in their bunk
beds
David did have a bedroom to himself
We decided to add a new master bedroom and a large
den
At the beginning of the project
I remember lying down on the new den foundation
With the boys one night
A slight breeze blew cool and soothing
The smells of the night were a delight
As we marveled at the sky above
The stars winked from the darkness
And the planets softly looked down
Pure magic it was
The renovation proved ideal
With Kent, Mark, and David each getting a bedroom of
their own
A fenced backyard was perfect for the kids
I recall them playing soccer back there
Mark, always fascinated with cooking,
Once barbecued for us in that yard
Kent was into reading
Mark was into mischief
Well, playful mischief
Oh, and cooking, tennis, and the saxophone
David was into soccer from four-years-old
One night the electricity flickered off

For more than an hour
Bored?
Not with Mark around
He brought out his saxophone
The one he played in the high school band
And preceded to play it as the candlelight danced to the tune
As we all sat at the dining table enjoying the concert
At 2311 Kent Street, Kent found his soulmate,
Jackie
In the ninth grade
Their love blossomed into marriage a few years later
Mark found love in high school
Cindy is her name
David married a few years after moving out
Michele is her name
Love all my daughters
OK, daughters-in-law
Back to Mark and Cindy
One day, when they were dating each other
Mark unexpectedly brought Cindy to the house
I had to hide since I was in my sleeping clothes
White drawers only
That taught me to wear something more than drawers until bedtime
Mark played tennis for Bryan High School
He was good at it
I loved watching him play
An aside
Cindy and Jackie teased me about my cereal habit
See, I kept the cereal in our upright freezer
Kent started nearby Texas A&M University
While still living at 2311 Kent Street
Kent, ever the environmentalist
I recall him arriving home from A&M on his trusty bicycle

Kent was co-masters of ceremonies for his high school talent show

Ever the jokesters, Kent and Ross King guided the show with expert timing

Kent soon moved out to a rent house peopled by a couple of roommates

He graduated from A&M and eventually got a master's degree from there

Mark moved out to attend the University of Houston culinary school

Which focused on management

And served as an excellent jumping-off point in his career

My wife and I went down to Houston on a special open house day

We toured the facility and saw Mark in culinary action

David and I read Charlotte's Web together when he was little

Before long he closed his eyes and dreamed

I can still see David on the soccer field from four years old to through his high school years

David looked good out there

Aggressive, competitive, and the ultimate team player

David left 2311 Kent Street for Alaska when he graduated high school

He was following his infant daughter

She was moved to Alaska by her mother and her parents

David graduated from the University of Alaska and soon married Michele

Whom he met at a restaurant where they both worked

At one time, Kent, Mark, and David all played soccer

It was a Saturday, and all three were playing games in three different fields at the same time

From one end of Bryan-College Station to the other
Mom and I did our best to see all three games
It was hectic, but we did it
My wife and I helped lead our church youth group for a
few years
While Kent, Mark, and David were participants
Occasionally, I would teach Sunday School as a
substitute teacher
I liked to be visual
One lesson included a passage from the Bible that
included a ram's horn
I borrowed one from a local taxidermist
I showed it in the class
And made a point the class did not forget
We once chaperoned a coed overnight event in the
fellowship hall
The whole night we guarded against hookups
We roamed the facility corralling the youth
Practically sweating with anxiety
We never chaperoned again
A couple of years in a row we hosted a youth weekend
retreat
At our house
The kids played games and conducted Bible studies in
our home
And heard speakers in the church fellowship hall
One year we caravanned as usual from the fellowship
hall
As we got home, another group of teens stopped at the
house
Thinking we were having a drinking party
Nope
No alcohol at the retreat
While at Kent Street, I began an unwanted side
journey
I started obsessing over my predicament

Fearing for my job and thinking I was not making
enough money
And feeling worthless
My wife did the bill paying and all the finances
We never discussed our finances
That would come back to haunt me
Because I was lost on my own
One day in my late 30s, I attempted to put my shoes on
Slipping a shoe on just any way suddenly no longer
worked for me
I tapped the floor with my foot
And attempted to put my shoe on
Not good enough
I tapped again
Not good enough
Finally, an agonizing few minutes later I got it exactly
right
And I slipped the shoe on
Next foot
Same tapping until I was satisfied I did it just right
It took at least ten minutes just to get my shoes on
I started doing this every day
I started checking everything
Especially the lock at the front door
And my truck door
I would turn to the front door key to lock it
Not good enough
I turned the key to unlock it to start over
I did this over and over until I thought it was just
right
The more I worked the lock the more frightened I
became
I bent the key a couple of times
The truck door was the same deal
My reason for all this maddening activity?

To avert dreadful things from happening to me and all those around me
I thought no one else had these thoughts
I knew this was not rational, but I couldn't stop
Mainly because I feared for my job
I would be more than lost if I lost it
Stuck on this planet with nowhere to go
And I thought I was being pressured by my bosses to quit
Overwhelmed, I sought help
Through work, I found a local mental health counselor
I was both depressed and suffering from what I learned was obsessive-compulsive disorder
I also learned that I was not the only one with this malady
Treatment?
No medicine for the depression
Just a pep talk
OCD?
A rubber band on my wrist
I was to pop it when I did those foolish things
This helped a little
She recommended no medicine for my OCD either
I now take medicine for my depression and OCD
In the meantime, my wife and I partnered with my brother, Arnold
In buying three fourplexes and two single-family homes
My wife handled showing the units and the bookkeeping
I oversaw lawn maintenance and upkeep
I painted one of the fourplex's exteriors during that time
All this with both of us working fulltime
We never talked about it
But I'm sure this was an incredible strain on both of us
Of course, we never talked about it

With my sons moved out, we soon confronted the stark reality
Living separate existences
Merely roommates
2311 Kent Street seemed too big and lonely
My wife had an excellent job at A&M, and I remained tied to my job
From which I felt much of the time I was one mistake away from losing
I felt a little jealous that she seemed to confidently move along
While I struggled, heavily
I know now I should have shared my plight with her
I was more at fault than her for the distance between
Mentally I was a mess
Here is what I remember
My wife once reminded me of a time
When she planned dinner for me at the house
I worked that day
The dining table was set

Food ready
My wife was waiting on me
I do not remember her telling me what she had planned
I did not call to tell her I would be late
I regret that and all my long work hours
I felt trapped in that job
Having no faith in my abilities to do anything else
So, I thought I had no other job prospects
I recall my wife lying on the bed sobbing from time to time
I was too numb and depressed to ask her why she was crying
Perhaps I knew
I stood in the kitchen

Listening as tears fell down her face
I never looked her in the eyes
And asked what's wrong, sweetheart
I just struggled alone hoping for magical relief
One weekend my wife traveled alone
To her brother's home in Mt. Pleasant, Texas
We usually visited him at least once a year
But she never went alone
Fearing the worst, I called her nearby sister
And expressed my feelings and fears
She suggested writing her a letter
I did, in shaky longhand
In it, I poured out my soul
Asking for a second chance
I left the letter on our bed
When she returned late on Sunday
We hardly spoke, as usual
She went quickly to bed
While I waited in the living room for a reaction
Pure silence for at least an hour
I peeked in and she was sound asleep, letter in hand
I slept on the couch
She never talked about the letter
I never asked her, fearing the response
Of course, the silence was an answer
The next day we talked briefly
I mean briefly
I asked her if we could start marriage counseling
"It's too late," she said
Should we divorce?
She nodded
Feeling most responsible for our predicament,
I said I would file
I mean I knew my demons --
My depression, my OCD, and my paranoia
The next afternoon as I prepared for my nightshift

My wife was already at work
I opened a bathroom cabinet door, looking for I do not know what
In the cabinet, I saw a box of rat poison
I panicked
Logic escaped me
She is trying to kill me, my confused mind concluded
I drove to the nearby medical clinic, searching for answers
Am I going to die?
Can they pump my stomach?
Doctors finally said I was not poisoned
But by then I felt I could not go home, to work
Or do anything but get away
I was in no shape to let the Eagle know what was happening
An ambulance transported me
To the psych ward in a hospital complex in Waco, Texas
There I stayed for about a week
A parade of doctors analyzed me
Once I sat in a room with student doctors
As they probed me with rooky questions
I never got a diagnosis
I may have had some medication while I was there
But nothing was prescribed
My sister-in-law brought me home to Bryan
My wife was home when I arrived
She never asked what happened
Or how I was feeling
No hug, no nothing
Maybe she feared me
Of where I just came from
Later, I did file
Not up for a fight, I told my lawyer to split everything 50-50

In 1999, the divorce was finalized
Ending our 30-year marriage
I moved out of 2311 Kent Street after we talked that
night
My faith?
I abandoned it
A deacon at Central Baptist Church
Ready ears would have listened to me
And church members would have prayed with me
I felt a failure in God's eyes
And much embarrassed
I did eventually meet with the chair of deacons
To explain my situation
We prayed
I asked to meet with the pastor
Which I did
We prayed
Thus began a scary, sad, and unsettling time in my
life
One thing weighing on me was I did not know how to do
my finances
Anyway, shortly after the divorce, I quit my job of 30
years and moved to Atlanta, Georgia
Where my brother, Arnold, and Kent lived
Arnold kept urging me to move there
My resignation from the Eagle was effective
immediately
My editor kept trying to get me to reconsider
I was well thought of at the Eagle
The advertising director
A middle-aged coworker who I highly respected
Came over to my desk after hearing the news
Big tears falling from his misty eyes
An impromptu going away party was thrown at a nearby
pub that afternoon

A few days later another going away party was held at a
local venue
I sensed the love and respect for me
This helped me tremendously
After the divorce, we began selling our rental
property
In Bryan, and one in College Station
2311 Kent Street also was sold as we separated our lives
completely
I said goodbye to 2311 Kent Street from Atlanta
I was there when I learned it sold
For a fair price, I thought
I have not returned to the house in many years
I have since retired and moved to St. Augustine,
Florida
I just found a photo of the house online
It looks great
Bright green grassed front yard
Quaint façade with its red brick and cream trim
A few large trees are missing
But everything still looks great
In ways, I miss that 2600-square-foot home
For a few years, we all seemed happy there
I may go back one day
As I recall the good, the bad, and the extremely ugly
Constructed in 1961, may the Kent Street house
Bring comfort and joy to other families
For another 60 years.

ATLANTA, GEORGIA

Atlanta, for many years, was for me
Both magical and fraught with challenges
Magical because of Atlanta's mystique
With its Civil War past
Professional sports
A major metropolitan newspaper
CNN
And the famous Peachtree Road Race
Also, it was where my big brother, Arnold
And, eventually, my oldest son, Kent, lived
Atlanta seemed a beacon of hope
A city where I dreamed of moving one day
An avid runner at one time,
I longed to run in the legendary Peachtree Road Race
A 10k on a section of the more legendary Peachtree
Road
One year in the '90s, my dream came true
I decided it was time
The family rode to Atlanta again to visit Arnold and for
me to run
On the day of the race, my heart beat faster and faster
As I stood among dozens of other runners waiting for the
start
Pow!
Came the report of the starting pistol
I jogged in place for what seemed like ten minutes
As I waited for the runners ahead of me to pass the
starting line
Finally, my turn came
And I slowly picked up the pace
Startled, I felt the brush of a runner rushing past me
This was just the first of many folks passing me by
I was out of my league, I thought

But I kept putting one New Balance ahead of the other
As I settled into a comfortable pace
I heard cheers of you can do it and great job from the
sidewalk crowd
A couple of times bands played as I ran by
A few times I passed exhausted runners
Up ahead I suddenly saw it
Heartbreak Hill
The make-or-break last rise just before the finish line
T-shirt soaked in the July Fourth morning sun
My legs turned to rubber
Each heartbeat banged my chest
My pace dipped to a crawl
The crowd roared encouragement
Almost there
I inched over the incline
Toward the decline and that coveted finish line
My spirits lifted
I began to lengthen my stride to a flat out run
I blazed past the finish line
I later found out Arnold's son, Michael
Then around 14 years old, finished soon enough
To draw an interview by a local TV channel
I knew Michael was running
But I expected to far surpass his time
Not
I never got my official time
But I think around 45 minutes
Do not recall Michael's time but I know it was better
than mine
He did not even train beforehand
That is youth for you
And one determined young man
When I finished, I got the equally famous T-shirt
After moving to Atlanta much later
I walked the road race with my wife, Debby, in 2008

And three years later with Kent
Those are beautiful memories
I have since stopped running. Partly my injured right
knee.
I walk now
Here is another dream of mine back then
I would leave the small university twin cities of Bryan
and College Station, Texas
Where I was born and raised
Where I grew a family and a profession
Atlanta planted hopes in my head
This bustling southern city set in storied Georgia
Atlanta also was home to a big-city newspaper
The Atlanta Journal
I was a reporter, then editor at the small Bryan-College
Station Eagle
For 30 years
And through those years, I fantasized about going to a
big metropolitan newspaper
The Atlanta Journal would be perfect, I thought
Arnold and Kent and their families seemed content in
Atlanta
For a time, Arnold was a neighbor to a business writer
for the Journal
I should apply
What could go wrong?
Much, according to my muddled bipolar brain
I always felt a little over my head, even at The Eagle
I just was not good enough
And when it came down to it, I knew I was stuck in my
hometown
Anyway, my first wife and I and the kids visited Arnold
during summer vacations
Kent and his wife, Jackie, moved to Atlanta in 1996
As the Summer Olympics raced-on there

I always harbored a sad feeling that I would never be
able to move to Atlanta
The thought intrigued me, while it also made me
nervous
It seemed impossible
In 1999, my life as I knew it came crashing down
My wife of 30 years wanted a divorce
We sold our real estate
I went from a guy with a majestic home and family
To out the 2311 Kent Street door
And looking for a place to live
At work, things were going downhill
My divorce was weighing on me, and my work suffered
I was making editing mistakes
I was business editor and in charge of the Golden Eagle
A monthly periodical for seniors
One day my editor called me into his office and told me
I was reassigned
Starting immediately
To a job I was best at
News Editor
What I had done successfully for many years before
But it was a night job
Shocked and disappointed, I quit that very day
I just couldn't go back to nights
The boss who reassigned me kept trying to get me to
reconsider
But my heart was no longer in The Eagle
Slowly the gravity of my decision hit me
But I was not about to go back there
I went to and from Atlanta a few times during this time
In my used Silverado pickup truck
I started a divorce recovery class at Mt. Paran Church of
God in the Atlanta area
Diane, my sister-in-law, urged me to attend
Thus, part of the reason for the trips to Atlanta

Meantime, Arnold urged me to move to Atlanta and start over
I joined him in his real estate business
Arnold and I took our share of the proceeds from the sale of the apartments
And bought several rental properties in a rebounding section of Atlanta
He and I did not know what we were getting into
I eventually packed up my pickup and headed to Atlanta for good
For a time, I had no permanent street address in Atlanta
My early work responsibility was to housesit Arnold's vacant houses he wanted to rent out
I moved to several houses, ranging from needing a lot of work to pristine ones
A stay in one of his vacant houses proved eventful
One day, a car pulled into the driveway and stayed and stayed parked there
A potential renter, I thought
I realized the driver was just sitting there in his car
Then I realized his head was bent down on the steering wheel, as if dead
I called 911
The fire rescue folks rushed over
They knocked loudly on the driver's side window
It took a while
Finally, the man stirred
He said he had fallen asleep, he later told me
Yes, the fire rescue team left, leaving the fellow at the house
Would you believe I ended up showing him the house?
He acted as if nothing had happened
He did not rent it
The cynic in me still believes he just wanted attention

During this time, I felt lonely and adrift
Having left my longtime job and longtime marriage
And not having a place to call my own
Yet grateful to Arnold for helping me get to Atlanta
With these moves, all my belongings stayed packed into the bed of my truck
Save my 32-inch TV I stored at one of Arnold's rental properties
My anchor was my brother, my son Kent, and the divorce recovery class
It was in that class I met Debby, my saving angel
I did not know anyone in Atlanta other than Arnold and his family
And a college classmate of Arnold's who also lived in Atlanta
I had met a friend of Arnold's wife on one of our vacations
The leader of the recovery class kept warning of the dangers of starting
A romantic relationship too soon
So, I never visited that acquaintance
Fearing devastating consequences
With Debby, love bloomed again in my life
She was pretty, smart, and caring
Just what I needed
We developed a tentative friendship
That grew into a beautiful marriage and life
I feel like I was kind of a rebel dating Debby
While still in the recovery class
Its leader kept saying "no" to significant relationships for us too soon
I couldn't help myself
Debby invited me to join her for a Thanksgiving meal
Then we sat together in church
Things gloriously progressed from there
I joined the church

61

Debby was already a member
We became active in the church where we were fed
spiritually
I did stay with my brother for a brief time
But I do not remember the sequence
After a brief time, I wore out my welcome
And I agreed to move out
It was then my duties changed
And I started the housesitting
I do not remember how all that went down
It was 22 years ago
After a while, I became a handyman for Arnold
I had done a few repairs around two of our houses in
Bryan
But up to then, I had spent the bulk of my time as a
journalist
That deficiency soon cost me my job with Arnold
By that time, I somehow managed to move to the Post
Apartments
Debby and I chose to live together there
No sex, but plenty of companionship
We decided to wait until we were married
I was content with that because I loved her
And I was scared anyway
Because I had never been with another woman
On the day of our wedding, I sat in the stylist's chair
Almost shaking with anxiety
I watched as the stylist deftly scissored my bangs
Those famous bangs from my first wedding
I made sure I had no "bites" out of them
Like happened in my first wedding
Satisfied, I watched as the stylist gave Debby a wedding
updo
My son, David, said I looked like a used car salesperson
I powered through anyway

Our wedding was held in my son, Kent's Bed &
Breakfast
There in Atlanta
From there, the story continues.

810 MOONLIT LANE

After the apartment, we bought the tri-level 810 Moonlit
Lane house
Debby and I did a ton of work on the house while we
were there
Repainting throughout, putting up crown molding
Tiling the kitchen and dining room floors, and replacing
the front door
We loved the Moonlit Lane house, but we hated the
stairs and the distance from our jobs
Debby was a registered nurse working in hospice
There my alcohol intake grew alarmingly
I began stopping in at a neighborhood bar on the way
home from work
Why I do not know
From sadness in knowing I couldn't work for Arnold
forever
My job future was bleak
But I was scared to look for something else
I would not stay late at the bar, and I drank a few beers
I just wanted to fit in where others fit in
I began drinking wine at home then
Lots of wine
Debby was concerned
Enough so that one day I watched as she poured out
All the wine in the house down the basement bathroom
sink
At some time there, I was talking to Arnold's wife,
Diane
And I expressed to her that I feared I was becoming an
alcoholic
I do not recall her reaction
I talked to Debby, who was very worried about me
And we both went to the psychiatrist

Monitoring my meds and pleaded for my plight
She recommended I check in for a weekend at a local facility
Specializing in alcohol abuse cases
I did
I spent a Friday and Saturday night there
Sitting in on group sessions
And conversing with fellow abusers
I never felt comfortable
Ashamed is what I most felt
Lacking a dramatic drinking story,
I must have seemed dull to the others
I did not have withdrawal symptoms
I quit cold turkey after that
Lesson learned
On Moonlit Lane my mania manifested
I bought 15 VCR documentaries on famous people
Winston Churchill and the like
I wanted to find their secret to life
Heaven knows I did not know it
Oh, we did not even have a VCR player at the time
My mania at work
One day, I'm cruising along on I-85
Still working
I spot a yellow taxicab up ahead
Something in my bipolar brain
Tells me I need to catch the cab
Because I need to talk to the passenger in it
No earthly idea why
That did not matter to my brain
Just follow the cab, fast
I spot the taxi up ahead and speed up
Just then, logic took over
I'm out of control
I phone my wife at work
In the middle of dealing with a patient

She rushes to answer
I'm chasing a cab
Go straight home! Debby says in a calm voice
I do
She saved my life by that reaction
It calmed me as then I knew what to do
We talked that evening when she got home
I could see the concern in her eyes
Back to the therapist, I went
The schizoaffective disorder was the therapist's
conclusion
That diagnosis stuck with me
Until we moved to Florida
Where a psychologist I was seeing
Said I was suffering from bipolar disorder
Oh, we planted a magnolia tree in the front yard of
Moonlit Lane
We drove by a year after we sold the house
And the magnolia appeared healthy and growing
No green thumbs us, we were proud of our singular
success
The house looked great
I recall we had our first Christmas tree there
Since we married
It reminds me of many good memories
Despite the awfulness of 810 Moonlit Lane.

Marlborough Drive

Soon after selling Moonlit Lane my brother laid me off
I went several months with no job while our bills piled
up
By then, we had moved to Marlborough Drive in
Tucker, an Atlanta suburb
Debby kept us afloat
Soon it all came to a dramatic conclusion
We filed for bankruptcy
We lost almost everything
To say this was a low point is to understate
Credit shot, me making no income
I desperately sought a new job
Going to Arnold's office
Where he let me search for job listings in the paper
At home, I searched the internet on job listing sites
Nothing in journalism
Nothing in anything I was qualified for
I tried newspapers again for three months
Working as editor of two small weeklies
It did not work
I was still burned out from The Eagle
And I never figured out the coverage area
I searched exhaustively for a job
Debby suggested I volunteer for a hospice
A hospice gives terminally ill patients
End-of-life comfort and care
I sat with a patient for a couple of hours
Simply talking to the patient
And providing companionship
One patient proved quite lively
A voracious talker herself
She saw my wedding ring and asked to see it
I tried and tried to distract her

But she was insistent
I took the ring off and handed it to her
Bad idea
She slipped the ring onto her finger
I waited a bit and I asked for it back
She just kept talking
About any and everything except the ring
Please give it back, I asked patiently
No dice
Please give it back
More talk
I need it back, I pleaded
Finally, she began taking it off
It would not budge
Her knuckle was large
I panicked
Should I get some soap and water?
Just then, she managed to slide the ring off
Whew!
That taught me a lesson
I did not fall for that one again
She was such a sweet little lady
I couldn't be mad at her
I sat with several precious people during this time
One day, Debby, a registered nurse working for a hospice
Urged me to become a certified nurse assistant
Debby worked with CNAs daily and knew their duties
They helped her tremendously, she said
A little reluctant, I finally decided to go all out
I had never worked in the medical field before
The title comes with certification by the state where you live
I passed the training and the certification test
What is the job description of a CNA?
CNAs work directly with patients and nurses,

Helping with the many physical and complex tasks for patient care
Some of the responsibilities include turning or moving patients
Bathing and changing diapers and assisting with feeding
With Debby's help, I found a job at the hospice where she worked
I worked with that company for seven years
I did what is called continuous care for the hospice
This means caring for one patient at a time in 12-hour shifts
I traveled to the patient
At homes or nursing homes or assisted living facilities
Continuous care is used when patients require extra monitoring
What is hospice?
Hospice is a type of medical care that gives seriously ill patients
And their loved ones
Meaningful time together
When the focus of care turns from active treatment
To comfort and quality of life near the end of life.
Hospice is not a place
Rather, it is a full range of services that put patients and families in control,
Giving them hope about their last days, weeks, and months together
One of my fears was a patient falling on my shift
I had heard horror stories about broken bones and worse
Once a frail male patient asked to go to the bathroom
I got him out of his bed, no problem
I held onto him as he shuffled forward
In an instant, he slid down to the floor
It was a soft fall, thank goodness
But a fall nonetheless
I raised the tall gentleman to his feet

And we proceeded to the bathroom
Without further incident
I reported the fall and sweated for my job
Nothing was said to me
I realized that other CNAs dealt with falls as well
I was hypercautious for the next seven years of my
employment
As a hospice CNA, I saw several patient's dying breath
After an obvious death, it is eerie to see what appears to
be breathing
In a semi-circle standing hand in hand
The family, the hospice doctor, and me
Pay respects to the 87-year-old patient
Who died moments before in her bed
The doctor leads in prayer
At the end of it, she hugs the family members
Everybody hugs, including me
I never grew accustomed to those deaths
They all touched me deeply
I thought of my own family and friends
And how I would feel seeing them lying there
I felt honored to care for my patients
I helped people in a tough time of their lives
The CNA job was a lifesaver
It gave me an honorable purpose
It helped keep my depression and OCD in check
And set me up for a fortuitous move to Florida
While at Marlborough Drive
I developed a love of writing poetry
It blossomed from my daughter-in-law, Michele
Looking me in the eyes
And asked me to author a poem for her newborn son,
Noah
I dabbled in poem writing before as a hobby
But I was truly honored when she asked this of me
I was surprised yet delighted at the request

70

Yes, I would, I said, wondering if I was up to the task
After much deliberation, here's what I produced

Noah, you with your 10 tippy toesies
May you be blessed with a future that is rosy
You are a sweet bundle of hiccups and love
Arriving on earth from God's Heaven above
May you always enjoy a cleansing bath
And may your feet always follow the righteous path
May you always strive to give love away
To parents, siblings, friends, and that special one someday
Give logic a whirl, but know that in the debate
It truly is faith that pries open many a gate
Enough of lofty thoughts from grandpa this noon
It is time for a cow to jump over the moon

This poem was written in 2013
The year of Noah's birth
Michele began compiling my poems through the years
Making them into a book each year from 2013 to the present
None of them are published outside of those personal books
Not sure how the public would react
I do have an email list of some 50 friends and relatives
That I send new poems to
Positive responses keep me motivated
Poetry corrals my thinking
Pushes me to create some small measure of positivity
I admit it is a selfish ambition
I get a real sense of accomplishment in my bones
Trying to outdo me with each new effort
Life on Marlborough Drive was soft and furry
What with our dogs Mocha and Princess
Providing love and companionship

Both were small
Mocha, a Pomeranian stayed nervous but sweet
Princess, a Cavalier King Charles Spaniel, proved the
most docile of the docile
They were especially comforting to Debby
They came along with us to two more houses
Houses I will mention in the next installment
We sold Marlborough Drive to a nice young couple
We drove by a year later
And it looked as great as we remembered.

753 BAHIA DRIVE

Socks
Multicolored
Warm to the touch
Fresh out of the dryer
I match and fold them as I stand in the laundry room
Next to my wife, Debby
She pulls the rest of the clothes from the dryer
Our eyes meet, and we smile
A perfect magic moment
On the couch in the Florida Room
Debby at one end
Me, on the other
Coffee cups to our lips
Silent we sit as morning breaks
I marvel at my good fortune
As I watch Debby enjoy that first cup
A perfect magic moment
Night falls
Time to go to sleep
I stand looking at Debby
She gazes at me
We move toward each other
And we gently kiss goodnight
A perfect magic moment
My life seems full of magic moments
How are they?
Perfect!
Yes, certain moments on 753 Bahia Drive in St.
Augustine, Florida
Proved magical
Yet other moments were not
We have had some struggles here too
For instance, in the first year here

My psychiatrist, who first diagnosed me with bipolar disorder
Thought because of possible long-term side effects
I should try discontinuing my Risperidone
A horrible idea as it turns out
Soon, I became almost impossible to live with
My wife, Debby, felt the brunt of my intense irritability
I couldn't stop speaking curtly to her
My mind relapsed
Into my old ways before Risperidone
I was on an antidepressant and a mood stabilizer
Not enough
Debby, ever my medical shepherd
Sensed the problem
I quickly went back on Risperidone
I evened back out after that
My heaviness and irritability vanished
This was quite a scare
That taught us to stay even more vigilant
Speaking of Debby
She most thoroughly watches over me and my moods
She has a sixth sense about me
If I get manic
She sets me straight
If I get depressed
She reminds me of our good fortune
I need help with my meds
She keeps all that straight
Debby blesses me daily with her loving presence
We arrived at 753 Bahia Drive by way of Lanier Spring Drive in Gainesville, Georgia
And Cornell in St. Augustine, Florida.
We lived for about a year in the Cornell house
A rental owned by Debby's sister, Sandra
Moving to Florida from Atlanta after retiring in late 2012

We itched to move into a place of our own in 2014.
We have lived in this quaint one-story, two-bedroom home ever since
It is painted white with deep blue shutters
Two palm trees and a giant oak dominate the front yard
The yard we finished out with all-native plants
We fell in love with this charmer on the first showing
We are close to the beach
Our sweet dog Sasha
Her tail wagging and her nose to the sand
Excitedly almost runs onto picturesque Crescent Beach
As Debby, with leash in hand, follows Sasha
A jet-black Maltese poodle
Sasha flies along with me delighting in our pup
All three of us leave precious sand footprints
We grow to love this mind-of-its-own doggie
Even more, as we watch her wavy fur blow in the breeze
We also watched in delight as the two dogs before Sasha
Ran and sniffed the same shoreline
We had Princess, a Cavalier King Charles, for 13 years
And our Pomeranian, Mocha, for 15 years
It is a short drive from the beach to 753 Bahia Drive
Where we marvel at our little air-conditioned house
The joy we feel here is magnificent
In 2012, while still in Atlanta, retirement beckoned
Until then, we never dreamed we would retire
We are so happy we did
While on Bahia, we joined Memorial Presbyterian Church
An ornate and beautiful church

Built by railroad magnate Henry Flagler over 100 years ago
Debby, who grew up in St. Augustine, attended the church during her childhood
We sometimes walk by her childhood home a block from the church
On her trip down memory lane
Once in Bahia, I joined, and Debby rejoined Memorial
It quickly became the bedrock of our existence
We became heavily involved
We became Stephen Ministers through the church
Stephen Ministry is a ministry of one-on-one Christian conversations with folks facing tough times
Such as divorce, loss of a loved one, or a loss of a job, and more
"Stephen Ministry grows the heart," says ministry leader, Amy Camp
At one time, I was a deacon and a docent there
A docent gives tours of the church and is an unofficial ambassador of Memorial
Bahia has proved a mecca for our five children and 16 grandchildren
The dining table awaits an army of sons and daughters-in-law
As well as a passel of beautiful grandchildren
A fresh-baked turkey rests fresh-carved in the kitchen
Wafting a sweet aroma
All the family at 753 Bahia Drive
Take their seats
Lord, bless this food for the nourishment of our bodies
Comes the prayer
Then an unspoken let's eat
And the culinary festivity begins
Clanks of forks provide the music
Loving conversations bring the lyrics
Our hearts burst with love

Covid-19 dominates the news as I write
We got vaccinated as soon as possible
Neighbors across the street contracted the virus
But survived without hospitalization
Several people in our church were infected
Our faith in God leads us to believe all will be well
Despite a new variant ravaging the world
Shades are drawn, Debby lies beside me
Naptime
I lay there trying for a short sleep
Then I hear it
There in the dark
A sound as if a serenading songbird lay next to me
A sweet whistling single note
It is drifting from my beautiful wife as she slumbers
Another perfect magic moment
I pray the Lord provides many more magic moments on
753 Bahia Drive
Here, I have learned how to deepen relationships
With my wife, family, friends, and church members
As well as the occasional stranger
I have learned true joy is birds on our backyard feeder
Little poignant times that sometimes go unnoticed
Debby and I continue to think of our passed-on puppies,
Princess and Mocha
And our sassy and wiggly streak of lightning, Sasha
Now I am almost done writing
I should rest my mind
Yes, it is nap time
I plan to dream of those perfect magic moments
Oh yes, one more thing
The Looks of Love
As I begin to stare
I become aware
Of your soft silver hair
And begin to compare

Your rosy cheeks
To all I seek
I wonder at your eyes
Blue-gray, they make me sigh
A sweet dimple in your lovely chin
Brings life to your happy grin
And hints at the light within
Your aura fascinates my inner being
When I look at you, I keep on seeing
My most beautiful bride
And pray you will stay by my side
The look of you gives me pride
Especially when I see
How you look at me
The looks of love, and praise be
We fit each other to a tee.

MY ROAD TO JOURNALISM

My road to journalism started in junior high on Brazos Street

In junior high, I wrote in English class a story about a girl who rode horses

I described the horse's mane and the girl's blond hair flowing in the wind

My teacher showed the story to my parents at an open house

In high school, I was fortunately enrolled in the school's journalism class

My brother and I moved back to Highway 21 during my junior and senior years

While there, my writing knowledge blossomed

Thanks to my teacher, Mrs. Edwards

She was a brilliant journalism instructor

She placed me on the school newspaper staff

I was sports editor, which is where Russell Autrey was the photographer

On the track team, this seemed a natural fit

Speaking of tracks

Russell still teases me about my four-track tape player

Mounted under the dashboard of my 1956 Ford

The player immediately grew obsolete when eight tracks
rolled in

Shortly after my purchase

For the paper, I covered all the sports and wrote about
them

In my column called From the Wall

I formed a deep friendship with all those in the class

But I lost track of them after leaving high school

When I entered Texas A&M University

Studying journalism

I graduated in 1971 with a bachelor of arts degree

In journalism with a minor in sociology

I married in 1969 and moved back into 126 Waverly

Where I joined the local newspaper part-time

 Before I graduated from A&M

I spent the next 30 years at that small The Eagle

I rose from a reporter covering surrounding small towns

To writing about the City of Bryan

I moved to news editor from there

Designing the layout of the paper

And editing and writing headlines for each issue

In the 70s, The Eagle moved to a new building

I went with it, still as the news editor

At the same time, the paper changed to a morning paper

That meant my deadline went to midnight daily

So, my years of night work began

In charge of getting the paper out on time,

My nerves remained on high alert

From the moment I walked into the building

Even past the printing of the issue

I got the first paper off the press

And scoured it to make sure it was perfect

The next day would be nerve-wracking too

Until I heard from my bosses

If a headline was inaccurate

Or the wrong stories were chosen

My nerves turned loose

And my heart jumped back into my chest

When I got the all-clear

That evening, the clock kept ticking toward midnight

We hold a news meeting early in the shift

Where the stories and photos are selected for the next
issue

I listened carefully and made suggestions

Also, in charge of the front page

I recommended stories from our wire services

The city editor made suggestions for local stories

The editor road herd on us all

Eventually, I grew weary of the night shift

And asked for work during daylight hours

At one point I was the religion editor

Then I became the business editor

My day turned more relaxed

I left the paper in 1999 to relocate to Atlanta

Where I began a career in hospice

My time in journalism was both exciting and terrifying

Exciting from the rush of a late-breaking story

Terrifying from the awesome responsibility

Of changing out the front page on or past the deadline

I do miss coworkers I grew to love during my Eagle
days

I miss the adrenaline-pumping times

The Eagle still flies

And that makes me happy

Now I simply enjoy my nest

In retirement bliss

Checking out St. Augustine, FL living

In a single-family home

From which I hope never to roam.

Still Eagling After All These Years

Welcome to my recurring newspaper newsroom dream
Outside, the newspaper building dapples with
moonbeams
And head-lighted cars zip along on the dark streets
Most inhabitants of Bryan-College Station, Texas, are
fast asleep
While others are enjoying the cities' nightlife, dancing to
bands
Dozens of The Eagle newspaper's silent sentinels –
newsstands
Keep a night-time vigil, awaiting their daily breakfast of
newsprint
In the newsroom, I sit bathed in the bright light of
fluorescents
Will I make the deadline for the paper's production?
Will readers love what they see? Does that story need
liposuction?
As I dream this night, two decades after leaving there, I
feel the adrenaline
Flowing through my mind and my fingers once again
The only trouble is as the clock on the wall is about to
strike midnight
My mind seizes up, and my fingers freeze in fright
I realize I left out a story that might win a Pulitzer Prize
At that moment, my deadline, I shiver, and I pop open
my eyes
Awake now, faces of former colleagues hover like
holographs
As I remember sharing with them breaking news and
many good laughs

Overall, in my 30 years in that newsroom, if push comes to shove
I think not having these dreams I would never dream of
So, let me tip my hat to all my talented newspaper friends
And throw in a wish that the newsroom action never ends.

Of late, we take ballroom dance lessons
We can rumba, cha-cha, foxtrot, tango, sway, and a couple more
Here is my take on the subject:

A Chance on Dance

My wife holds a vision
She wants it to evolve into my vision
It is a dream for us to learn to dance
I love her, so I take the chance
We join a nearby dance class
Yes, that part comes from past
Shawn, our instructor, proves patient
As well as lenient
In the first month, we learn
To take a turn
At the Rumba quickstep
A dance with pep
I search for the beat
To move with my two left feet
After a while, I find my right foot
But the Rumba pattern I forsook
Wife Debby catches on quick
I dance not a lick
Oh, maybe a little bit
As I pit
My mind against my body
Soon we are not too shoddy
Next comes the learning of the waltz
Similar patterns as we enter talks
With Shawn about the waltzing stance
Though it looks difficult at first glance

My extra left foot returns
But at least the calories it burns
We almost master the dance
Next, we advance
To the cha-cha moves
See what this proves
Our visions set
I do not forget
We took a chance on dance
With more than a glance
I still need a little persuading
But my anxiety is fading
I see smooth moves ahead
As to dance contests, we head.
Now let me continue after a short interlude
With this little rhyme about this love of mine.
Though it may seem, it is not a dream
But a cherished new tradition.

A Sway to Stay

As we sway
To a sweet song today
We hold each other tight
And dance in the morning light
In each other's arms, we find
Love that does bind
Each softly beating heart
Will we never part
As the world
Continues to swirl
Two gentle souls silently sway
In our loving way
These magic moments just passed
Will forever last
As our love blossoms more
We then recall our time on the shore
You, barefoot in the sand
With our puppy as we planned
Our love joyously expands
As ocean waves begin to sway
Our hearts entwine
And engulf us in the divine.

Epilogue

What's it all about?

First, let me state.

Sometimes I get radical.

I change brands of toothpaste to generic.

I dress like Mrs. Doubtfire, wig and dress and all

For a Halloween costume contest.

I won even with my 50ish face giving women's looks a bad look.

I challenge myself to write poetry, starting in my late 40s.

I set out to write my memoir in a series of long poems

I mix shorter poems with the long poems

Most importantly, I take a chance on telling my bipolar story

As they say, wicked warts and all

So back to what life is all about

For me, it is love

And a serious dash of bipolar disorder.

My Bipolar Heart

Bipolar runs in the brain
That is the one refrain
Here is my take
This point I want to make
My heart
Is a part
Of this wacky swirl
In my bipolar world
It is with me all day long
It keeps me going strong
It supplies the blood
To my little brain, that could
Overcome my plight
With meds and some insight
My heart is full
With a little pull
Toward knowing
That I am growing
More focused each day
On my heart's gentle way
To quiet my brain
Of wrestling away my pain
So that I begin to gain
And even retain
A point of hope
As I begin to cope
My bipolar heart knows well
The things I could tell
But at this hour
It's loving power
Rocks me in a cradle
Which makes me more than able
To lean on my higher power
And my wife, Debby, every hour.
And …

The Mercy of the Mind

Lord, grant me mercy now
As I wonder how
You love me so
Yet, this I know
You've touched my mind
With your love so kind
And unswirled the mystery
Of my mental history
You took away
My need to pay
For miracles of my mind
Now I find
I'm no longer in a bind
You answered my prayers
You helped me climb the stairs
Toward a lifting light
That brings delight
And lets me know
You're more than a show
Thank you for your mercy on me
With it, I found the courage to break free.

Then there are the mysteries.

Mysteries Among Us

Everywhere a mystery
Throughout history
I ponder much
On Jesus's gentle touch
Why does He hold to me
Despite my attempts to flee
Back in the day
I fretted over my stay
On this mystery ride
Featuring some wide-eyed
Twists and turns
Some fast and slow burns
Full of mysteries of why
Time begins to fly
The older we get
And in our ways, we get set
Why words sometimes
Soak us in good times
Why other times
Words suppress
And create stress
The mystery of the search for power
That leads to bickering and wars every hour
On the other hand, I suggest
One mystery proves the best
It brings on a noble quest
For peace and permanence
In the glorious firmament
I speak of love for sure
The kind that is timeless and pure

We will know one day
About all the mysteries in the play
When we pass beyond
This worldly bond
Until then
Let us live among God's mystery pages
In His book of the ages.

Another mystery to me is grace
That beautiful gift from God.

Grace Chases Me

Looking at my life today

I must faithfully say

God's grace chases me

Although I do not always see

Such a wonder

That seems like thunder

In the distance

Since in this instance

God's grace chases me

To set me free

From my mistakes

He lifts me and takes

Me to a loving place

Yes, a state of grace

I love the chases

For burdens, He erases

My part hinges on me

Accepting His gift with glee

That is His plea

And I say glory be

As for comfort and peace

They wash over me with ease.

I hold some thoughts on prayer

We Will Pray

When the sunshine comes our way
We will pray
When the darkness comes one day
We will pray
Some will say
It's silly to pray
I say no way
I feel His heartbeat
Coming to steady my feet
When I pray
That's what I say
So, we will pray
Come night or day
I believe this is the way
To help us stay
On a straight line
Toward the ties that bind
That's what I find
As we begin to pray
Life moves beyond the fray
To the eternal
Away from the external
So, we will pray
Until the judgment day
And then there is my faith journey.

Road to Faith

I learned early

Life can give you surely

Roads to follow

Either fast or slow

Slow is my style

Moving all the while

Down a road I chose

Where it leads, only God knows

It took me through thicket and thorn

Yet, it showed me why I was born

At times the road seemed to end

But Jesus became my friend

I admit not at first

Despite my thirst

For freedom from dark days

That seemed a hopeless maze

Poor me, I used to think

Until one day, I began to blink

Which cleared my eyes

And I dropped my disguise

I opened up about my mental wounds

Insights and medicine helped me soon

Road hazards still roll up now and again

My new driver warns me as a friend

And we drive through them

As we do, I touch the hem

Of my holy driver as we smile

Knowing we will be riding for many a mile.

As for meaning in my life
I sometimes take a whimsical look

The Meaning of Life: Fly a Kite

I watched people breathe

Their last many times

In my hospice-nursing days

On that deathbed lies a life

Once vibrant and loving

Now their body is closed into one room

Some given painkilling drugs

Some, peacefully waiting

Of course, sometimes death

Arrives swiftly as in an accident

Or a heart attack and such

Was there meaning to those lives?

I say the departed's love changes form

I say their love in the atmosphere

Lifts kites

I believe in souls as much as kites

As kites glide and slide

I say souls float and fly

And while they are at it

Condition air with affection

For me, through days of giving love

And receiving it with joy

I find meaning through that sweet

Unequaled tug of love in myself

Finding that love in my soul

Is my quest

Now, who holds the string to my kite?

God helps me ride the wind

Yes, souls and kites

Life on strings

Tethering beings

Among the mystery of things

Like the fabulous feel of love

And the sight of kites lifted by soaring souls

That is how I see it from here

Floating above St. Augustine Beach

My soul soaked with a lot of love and sunscreen.

I believe those souls end up in heaven

With many magnitudes of companionship and love
Here are my thoughts on the subject
More thoughts on life

In a Twinkling

Stardust softly falls upon us
Every dazzling day
At night the source
Of that celestial substance twinkles away

Every precious moment of time
Showers down on humankind
Unseen with design most divine
A spray so refreshing from God's twinkler system

Man lifts longing eyes to that night
Having heard from scientists, women, and men
That stardust falls on us, even when out of sight
And as daylight nuzzles in

So, while I gaze up into sunny blue
Or almost lightless dark-black sky
I feel stardust inspires us to pursue
Love and laughter to quiet the baby's cry

To find the fine in stardust
Arranged for a flash of time
Into mortal sculptures that must
Return to stardust forever refined

The fall of stardust
Touches us lightly, invisibly
The sparkling dust must
Depart as life's dusk begins to gather

To lift our souls into the sky of delight
Where it meets with other loving stars
Stardust returns to stars this night
To twinkle anew for you and me.

My Heaven

I am a poet
This writing may show it
I want to talk about heaven
Using the tools I was given
I mean my soul and my mind
And my capacity to be kind
Jesus speaks of life eternal
And here I want to journal
About life after death
It is my ultimate quest
For if true
I will find you in the blue
Somewhere among the stars
Where God and Jesus are
I know I will turn to ash in the fire
Cremation is my desire
But where to then?
I do not think that is the end
There's been some anecdotal proof
So, I know it is not a spoof
And then there is what precious Jesus said
We will only be dead
To our earthly bodies, for sure
Which provides a hopeful allure
One that sets my heart astir
For I believe I will see
All those who mean so much to me
Yes, I am a poet
At least I think I know it
And as a poet, I know it must be true
That this earthly veil I will see right through
To the joyous vision of you.

Another take on heaven

Faith in a Heaven

What happens when my heart beats its last beat?
Whether in a disaster or at home in my living-room seat
Does my body transform into a new body in the
heavenly realm?
And do God, Jesus, and the saints give speeches?
As I face mortality, these questions come to mind
And other possibilities that are less than kind
Am I simply a computer that switches off when I die?
Or is there a burning hell in which I might lie?
Of late, I am something of a seeker
Reading this and that and listening to a speaker
Before retiring, I worked with patients who were dying
I watched several peacefully slip away as they were
relying upon
On God to pass them into heaven as they perceived it
And trusted they would not fall into the fiery pit
Sometimes I would tell the grieving family that the
loved one
Was in a better place, their time on earth over and done
That helped some, but others felt deceived
They prayed for healing, and they believed
A loving God would make their loved one whole
But despite their pleas, God stole
Back their mother, father, daughter, or son
It tugged at my heart for the loss of their loved ones
As I look now at those lives that passed
I wonder a little if my faith will last
When it is time for my life to become part of the past
Will I see loved ones who went before me?
In my hospice work, I learned some dying people see
Dead relatives or friends coming to talk with them

And in near-death experiences, it is more than a whim
Science and religion remain at odds on heaven as an
entity
But for me at this moment, it is faith in heaven that
brings me the serenity
To love and laugh and sometimes cry
Just knowing of that place in the sky.

What am I to poetry?

A Builder

Am I a builder?
Not in the regular sense
But in poetry
I build a skeleton
Of, hopefully, good bones
As for the skin of the skeleton
I think of the skin I'm in
And craft eyes and ears
And working arms and legs
If truly well done
A heartbeat within
Animates

Now my days are delightfully spent
With Debby and our dog Sasha
Here is a typical day

Other Selected Poems

A Morning in My Life

What time is it?
6:30 in the morning
My eyes blink open
As the dream, I was dreaming
Flies away from my waking mind
Night-dark swallows the bedroom
As the mystery of the morning unveils
A new day of little adventures
Or as yet unforeseen big adventures
God knows
But when will He let me know
Adds to the daily surprises
I shuffle to the Florida room and take in the darkness
That watches me through the large windows
I begin to think about poetry
Will I write a poem today?
I wrestle with the possibilities
I couch-sit alone for my wife will rise an hour or so later
I check the news on my phone
And YouTube something meaningful
I marvel at the bright sun as it flashes through the blinds
Rising to alert me to the coming excitement
Sure enough, our doggie Sasha flies in
With a lightning leap, she lands beside me on the couch
Wife Debby soon follows, and we kiss good morning
I take Sasha out to do her morning business

And we all descend on that same couch
For a time of poetry reading, reflection, and a devotional
Then I continue thinking of subjects for a poem
All this to say, I love my mornings
I treasure every one of them.

An Ordinary Life

An ordinary life

Seldom free from strife

Lean on luxuries in one sense

Full of love luxuries that grow immense

One where inward I call

To that innermost self of all

Where ordinary gets lauded

Little things applauded

I see ordinary quite clearly

As the miracles within me

I rise each morning

Before the dawning

To sit and ponder

How my life fills with wonder

And an exquisite blend

Of I love you and amen

Little did I know until now

Just how

An ordinary life satisfies

And justifies

Getting out of the way

Of myself each day

And revel in just being

Where I am seeing

Hearts so extraordinary

I would never call them ordinary.

Some things I love

I Love

Socks

Rocks

Clocks

Cars

Peanut butter jars

Mars

Stars

Smores

Sweet snores

God

Cod

My wife

Retirement life

Childhood

Car hoods

Sunsets

Pets

Sunrises

Compromises

Companionships

Sailing ships

Children

Grandchildren

Friends

Amends

Heaven

What we're given

Time

And rhyme

Sublime!

A Smile

A smile lifts
Brings shifts
In hearts
Finds the best parts
Of life's elations
In all translations
So, let a smile slip out
Show it all about
Let it be real
There is the appeal
Lose the pride
Deep inside
And compile
A book of smiles
Yes, a smile lifts
It is one of God's gifts
And it is free
Let all come and see.

Building Futures:
Habitat for Humanity

With every hammer of a nail
Love will prevail
With each burring of a saw
One stands in awe
Of work done here
For the world to hear
Of a new home under construction
Let this be a new direction
For the recipients
As it is part of the ingredients
For a future bright
With a fresh living room insight
Bless the owners of this new abode
For many years down the road
Blessings and love.

Mother's Day Reflections

I look forward each year
To Mother's Day, just short of a tear
My emotions are juiced
Given a joyous boost
When I recall
Days of my youth and all
I love my mother who died when I was one
Wanted to make her proud I was her son
I take particular note
In the handwritten poem, she wrote
That braced me for a life
Of both joy and strife
Of ups and downs
My love more than abounds
For my mother, so fondly spoken of
Family and friends assure me she resides above
With my dad in a bond of love
OK, sometimes that tear does fall
For little and big events, I recall
She was missed in my life after all
My older brother also finds space
To put her in a regal place
As we share our hearts
With our mother, who gave us our start
Happy Mother's Day, mother!
You are like no other
So, throughout our years
For her, I feel she wants no tears
Even now, I follow her call
To find joy in life above all.

When the Storm Comes

When the storm rages
Check your gauges
That measures your attitude
And decide to seek gratitude
Since God is a light unto thee
That shines your way free
From the roiling sea
Let us forever
Make courage your endeavor
So, when a storm blasts your way
Landing you in the fray
Full of tumult and trials
Where seldom come smiles
Let me remind
One day you will find
Thunder and rain
No longer remain
As God creates a rainbow
Amidst the clouds below.

Jesus Come Down

Jesus come down
And still, the sound
Of bombs all around
Still, the subtle sound
Of tears falling on frightened cheeks
As the Devil speaks
With his torching tongue
Right there among
His blazing guns
Jesus come down
Still, the battling hearts
That is where it starts
Steady the heroes' hands
As they thwart the Devil's plans
Jesus come down
And help peace resound
Throughout Ukraine land
As you take their outstretched hand.

Finding Peace and Trust

Recently we sat down
While on the grounds
Of a nearby park
Today, memories they spark
On a green-painted lawn swing
We sat as our troubles took wing
I looked at my wife
And thought, what a great life
We swung luxuriously slow
As a gentle breeze began to blow
There on Debby's lap sat
Our beloved doggy Sasha who knows where it is at
For she finds joy in all
Winter, spring, summer, and fall
As we swung, we smelled
A watery wind that compelled
We to spot boats on the water
Racing by as they ought to
Lush green grass expands before us
As we find something to trust
We trust the giant oaks above
Casting shadows of love
We trust the sound of laughter
In the nearby swimming pool just after
Someone splashes a cannonball jump
We trust the wildflower field just there
Giving hope for a world beyond compare
We trust the small playground
We hear the sound of kids on the merry-go-round
We trust the puffy clouds in the sky
Bringing pleasure to the eye

Swinging there, we trust our thoughts to stay
In loving memory of this shared day
It is one of those moments we did not want to end
In a place that becomes a friend
Who brought us peace
And a joyous ease.

Boundless

Creativity is personal
It is deep within yourself
It is where love lies
Where your spirit comes forth
To rouse your centering thoughts
Into something boundless
Ever reaching further and further
Into loving air
Where peace and fulfillment abound
Beyond all dimensions
Boundless it is
Where limiting thoughts vanish
And you fly
It is not as if you try
Instead, you let life flow
In ways never thought of
In the vast new knowledge
Of your inner love and peace
Boundless it goes
Toward unknown heights
As your creativity lights
Not so much writing or art and such
But pure living correctly
Beyond what we thought
All boundless it is
Yes, boundless as we give
Our searching light to others
For we might share
This brave new boundlessness we feel
It holds such an appeal.

Where Am I From?

I could say I am from Bryan, Texas
Where am I from, down deep?
I am from a place called love
Derived from mixing of DNA
I am from a portion of the heavens
Where God plays his heroic part
In piecing together human life
I am from a miracle
That spans the ages
At once here and also, there
So, in a way, I am from everywhere
And I am still here and there
Places of sights and sounds
Yet silence abounds.

Future World

Today I seek
To work hard and long
This world to fix
In my little way
I see possibilities
If I try to find
Bits and pieces
Of joyous actions
That fit together
Into a perfect puzzle
Of brilliant potential
Let me, dear Lord
Give you your due
In creating a future world
Full of worthwhile living
I pledge to do my part
As today I start
On the road to paving the way
To respect and joy as I pray.

Looking for Beauty

Looking high and low
Don't you know
For beauty in you
And I found it too
Rising above
In beautiful love
You have brought me joy untold
As our lives beautifully unfold
Now, as the days go by
As they fly
Let the beauty in us
Also, help us trust
Not just in the beauty of our own
But in the beauty of the Son
Who brings sunshine out of the rain
And puts us on the golden train
To joy and wonder
And always stay under
His beautiful protection
May we of beauty be a reflection
Of Jesus's love and devotion
As we check our emotions
Let us lean on the everlasting arms
Where there are no alarms
Show us how your beauty flows
Within us, sweet and slow

Why I Love Writing Poetry

Days go by, and I recall
Places without rhyme at all
And my unsettled mind
Looks for a better time
Poetry, for me, bubbles up so fine

More often than not
Poetry calms my nerves once set in knots
Oh, what fun it is to unfold
As my laptop and I turn bold

I should say it also serves
Besides calming my nerves
To fill that spot
In my soul, that is not
Quite content
Poetry is heaven sent
And all seems right
As rhythm and rhyme become a delight

Now, as I write
I keep my sights
On saying something relevant
Like the weight of an elephant
And maybe something deeper
Like being my brother's keeper

Oh, I love to rhyme
But not every time
Rhythm is a friend of mine
I strive for the likes of fine wine

Yet sometimes it is the likes of soda pop
And sometimes out I opt
To start again
Until the poem is my friend

Now it is time to come to a close
And begin my repose
My next poem? Heaven knows.

A Solid Rock

I found a solid rock
That holds me around the clock
It steadies my feet
As I relinquish defeat
And take a stand
As I take your nail-scarred hand
And form a plan
That is more than grand
You are a solid rock
That tends your flock
In the kindest way
Now, let me say
You are a hero of mine
You are my most loving find
No, you found me
And now I see
A clear road
That you bestowed
On this soul of me
That you set free
To stand not alone
On the precious stone
Now, on the solid rock, I stand
All other ground is sinking sand.

A Quiet Bird

I am a quiet bird
To chirp loudly seems absurd
I like to stay in my nest
To do otherwise, I protest
I like the worm
But to rise early makes me squirm
I would rather read
A particular reed
Rather than flap about
And chirp and shout
I like solo flights
Among the kites
No hen parties for me
Small chitter-chats I do not see
I like time alone
Ever since grown
Do not get me wrong
Let me say this strong
I love my time staying free
As long as I can sit with you, my little chickadee
Yes, I am a quiet bird
More than most by a third.

Who is in Control?

You can throw out
All kinds of a shout
As to who or what
Is in control of our lot
Is it fate
That makes us debate
Where guidance comes
And allows us to become
Twisted up lab mice
That seems to entice
Us away from clarity
Where decisiveness is a rarity
Here is my take
It is a mistake
To think life willy-nilly
That is silly
I say God has our back
Now, let me unpack
This thought of mine
Life is controlled by the divine
Although sometimes it does not make sense
We get worried and tense
God has an ultimate plan
We do not fully understand
Yet, it has a flow
From here, do you know where to go?
Or do you harbor other plans
Such as giving fate a clap of the hands?
As for me, I see
God is in control and sets me free.

Spreading Seeds

Think of this
What would we miss
If we stay inside
And hide
Our talents and treasure
Beyond all measure
Would we fail to plant
The seeds God continues to grant
To each of us
Let us discuss
The opportunities that abound
That surely resound
In spreading the seeds
Of honorable deeds
The kinds that define
This world of yours and mine
Now is the time
To bury deep
Seeds that sleep
To sprout anew
Amidst the golden dew
As for me,
I came to see
Daily, I have the possibility
To the best of my ability
To plant more seeds
Honoring the world that pleads
For more kindness and love
And the peace of a dove

Dear Jesus

Dear Jesus
Bless you and all you did
And all you do
I lay before you my mental issues
From depression to mania to OCD
Lift me from this madness
As you do every minute that I live
Praise to you for helping me through
With your loving kindness
And your spirit-raising
Thank you for the medication
That helps in the fight
I pray you rescue
All those in mental darkness
Move them from desperation
To delight
I pray for all souls
Seeking
Seeking
Amen

Not Knowing

Sometimes
Probably best
To not know
For sure
Your last day
Your last hour
Your last breath
But know this
It comes
I lay my life
Before God
As a testimony
Of good and bad
Assumptions
Let that final day
Be a blessing
I don't want to know more
Until I land on heaven's shore.

Among the Meek

Daily I seek
To remain among the meek
I understand
One day the meek will be in demand
As they the meek shall inherit
The earth and they will share it
With those of all stripes
Yes, people of all types
Here is what I pray
Let me stay
Among the meek
That is what I seek
Let me walk
And silence the talk
Of tooting my own horn
From night till the morn
Let me see
The purpose in me
For sure, I pray
I find a way
To always stay
Among the meek
That is what I seek
To stay humble ever
Boastful never
Let me bow down
With a whisper sound
That gives thanks
That I strive for the ranks
Of the meekest of the meek
That is what I seek.

Shadows

Shadows are versatile
They can form long or short
They are sun and moon-driven
They dance along
With the stealth of a cat
I see mine
You see yours
Blistering days
Do not bother shadows
The cool of the night
Sometimes brings moonbeam shadows
At times, I lose my shadow
In the gloriousness of shade
I named my shadow Billy Two
I shake his hand
And he shakes back
When I am feeling athletic
We shadowbox
I miss Billy Two
When I am inside
For he is my twin
I love to see it over and again
Without the shadow of a doubt

Joy and Peace

Let us think
Of the true link
Between laughter
And the ever after
Between peace
And the release
Of hurtful noise
As we poise
For better days
And better ways
To find peace and joy
Here is something to employ
Let us look within
And forget the spin
From within, let us flower
As we lean on a higher power
Let joy and peace ring out
From our loving hearts without
Yes, let us be about
Finding the route
For truly fruitful days
Let us count the ways
To express
Our joy and happiness
Which leads to a peaceful clime
A place for all time.

If the Storm Comes

If the storm rages
Check your gauges
That measures your attitude
And decide to seek gratitude
Since God is a light unto thee
That shines your way to see
From the roiling sea
Let us forever
Make courage your endeavor
So, if a storm blasts your way
Landing you in the fray
Full of tumult and trials
Where seldom come smiles
Let me remind
One day you will find
A beautiful rainbow
That is what I know.

Comfort Call

When you find yourself
Out among the stars
Seeing the star-blinks
God winks
And draws you near
To whisper in your ear
Christ is here
Christ is here
Christ seeks to start
Spreading His love wings over your heart
And when you are on earth
Christ still sees your worth
So, when you need a comfort call
Christ is there to cover you all
With his soft outspread wings
While an angel sings.

Rainy Day Romantic

You wake up, and the day is cloudy
Now, of course, you could be pouty
You could let out a bleepity bleep
Or sulk without so much as a peep
But for all your complaining, nothing will change
Unless the forecast you could rearrange
Barring that, you might open up your mind
To thoughts of a romantic day, if you will be so kind
A cloudy day can bring the stuff of romance
If you will take a moment and give it a chance
One option is as rain clouds billow
Lay your head back on your pillow
Another is to take a walk in that rain
A giant umbrella will help you refrain
From drenching pretty hairdos as you walk
And allow for a long romantic walk
If that sounds a little too outrageous
Go to a museum; it is not so dangerous
Or how about a movie of a story of love
As raindrops splash down from above
The romantic in me says such a cloudy day
It turns out memorable if you decide to play.

A Voice

A tiny voice resides deep in me
It has made itself at home; it does not flee
Sometimes its words are sweet to my ear
Other times I do not even seem to hear
It is a voice that rings down through the ages
It remains wise as the battle rages
And it is in a language tailored to my ears
It speaks out through my trials and fears
I believe it is Jesus, that radical peacemaker
Whose voice gives counsel; he is not a taker
The historical record of this voice may be confusing
To some, the conflicting details are amusing
If I took all that seriously, my thoughts might bend
Suffice for me to believe that that helping voice will
forever send
Loving messages to me and others throughout eternity
Call me out of touch with the era of modernity
I will never deny I hear a knowing voice
And maybe you will listen too; it is up to you.

When the Light Shines

Ever feel a symphony in your soul?
It is like violins playing or a bell beginning to toll
Sometimes it comes on slowly
Other times it hits you quite boldly
A quick flash like a bolt of lightning
Something shows up that is enlightening
It is a spot in life where creative juices begin to flow
And the spinning thoughts start to slow
Your focus becomes laser beamish
If you step back, you might get squeamish
Best to go with the feeling, for it might not last long
I say, follow your heart and sing a new song

Just Do Not Give Up

As trials
Begin to pile
And the sun seems to set
To bring more darkness yet
Think of this
Please, let it rest
As your pain begins to grow
Here is what I know
God reigns
Through all your stress and strains
Give all to Jesus
He's here to please us
With a message of hope
That forges a way to cope
To break the chains
Of what remains
Right before you
Letting you know what to do
Jesus is the one that is true
Just don't give up
And remember Jesus and His loving cup.

Autumn Thoughts

Color-rich leaves float and flutter
Hardly a forest sound do they utter
Down they fall on the crispy-cooled ground
On which in spring new life will abound
Reflecting on my life, I see myself standing
Among the leaves of my past where I had hard landings
And now, as I stand in life's autumn air
I think did I do well or only fair?
The answer to that is for others who always debated
On this fall day, to me, it seems less complicated
I look back now through all the circumstances
And believe that I, at last, took the absolute right
chances
My wife and I took a chance by retiring from our careers
Rather than work on it for many years
We leaped together into this uncharted season
And began to do fun things for no particular reason
So far, we're whistling a happy tune
As we walk hand-in-hand beneath that old harvest moon.

No Sweat

I do not remember the first time I sweated
I mean T-shirt soaking
Forehead dripping
Down through eyebrows
Down past cheeks
Leaving salt deposits on the tongue sweat
I do not remember sweating when
In the side yard in an old vacated flower bed
Playing in the Texas dirt with my plastic soldiers
I do not remember sweating
When I slammed into the house
While learning to ride a bike
I did not even think much of sweat
Until air-conditioning
Slowly crept into neighborhoods
And businesses and public schools
In elementary school, I sat at my desk
Cross-legged and looking out
Open windows
Longing for recess
A recess outdoors where Texas heat
Surrounded me at dodge ball
I do not remember noticing the heat
But when word got out about the cooling machines
I began feeling the heat in the house
That suddenly was always there
But never noticed before
At first, I was unaware of the advantages
Of the early air-conditioners
It did not matter
We could not afford one anyway
I do not remember when I first
Slept without sweat

As a magical machine
Blew cool breath I had ever known
The brilliance of central air fascinated me
Both heat and cool at the twist of a dial
Air-conditioning in a car?
What a miracle!
To me, air-conditioners possess a beautiful aroma
Flowing from the strategically placed vents
Air-conditioning changed my life for the good
I push the digital thermostat to set my desired
temperature
And sleep as I must have as a baby
What is the best part of air-conditioning?
No sweat, of course.

Church Ouch

Greeted at the church door with a bulletin and a smile
Folks seem glad for us to stop by for a while
Inside, this world is something different
Subtle things and things that are significant
The nose senses the aroma of aged wood
No doubt carved with the artisans' hands that did better
than they could
As we settle in by picking one of the timeworn pews
The air is thick with echoes of past sermons and excited
I do's
And the exhilarating sound of the pipe organ soaring to
ceiling and sky
Then there's me as I sink into thoughts that bring me to
I
I get too comfortable, and I hide behind sleep-closed
eyes
As the clergyman preaches about life's little surprises
Suddenly, an elbow nudge from my wife makes my eyes
pop wide open
To see and hear what I needed and to remind me to keep
on hopin'
For the things that I don't always seem to know
That it takes a pastor to show
That is what God did for me down deep in my soul
And about that Jesus man who, with me, continually
strolls
By the way, pastor, please don't be alarmed
The sleep is not you, for you have passion and charm
My big fear as I admit this error
Is that next Sunday I will once again feel the elbow of
terror.

She Strikes Again

I know you know, dear pastor, that I'm on retirement
time

And, in the spare of it, I try to knock out a little rhythm
and rhyme

Last week, I was feeling repentful

I hope you won't be highly resentful

I wrote a little poem in which I confess

That sometimes, during the sermon, I get unsolicited
rest

I catch myself at times, but other times there is this quick
nudge

Back awake, I first think of my battle to slow down on
the fudge

Then I tune back into your soft and subtle voice

And I see being here was an excellent choice

Before I take fingers from the keyboard, I want you to
know

I saw all of your sermon this Sunday with my mind in
tow

I wrote in the bulletin you saying God is working his
purpose out

Due to my writing, my wife thought I was making
another egregious error

She gave me a shot from her elbow of terror

She thought, on the bulletin, I was working on a new
poem

Please forgive me for again running astray, busting the
decorum

I pray that through your new glasses, you can see your
way

To please forgive this ol' Texas boy one of these days .

A Reunion

St. Augustine Florida, 2013
To me, there's nothing grander
Than to be an interested bystander
Looking on at a 50-year reunion
Of high-school buds remembering their union
Back in the days when life was simpler
Or, at least it appeared that way until the face got pimplier
And when the school work got tougher
And perhaps relationships got rougher
But for many to remember those days
Brings a blissful feeling that stays
For, I looked on at this party with awe
As all the classmates' little reunions I saw
My wife gave and got dozens of hugs
Each friendship rekindled gives my heart tugs
For this night, I was not quite prepared
To see all this love freely shared
Here's what this bystander took from all this
That night, my wife and I had a much sweeter goodnight kiss.

Moment by Moment

I'm praying for this particular moment of mine
To become a well-used passage of time
Let it prove a moment of challenge or growth
Perhaps with proper work, it could be both
Now, as I ready myself to find lines that rhyme
I decide to write about how I want my moments to be sublime
I want to look in awe at a grandchild's smile
And concentrate on this little one's style
I want to watch as my wife pets a pet
It makes me know my mind is set
On this Florida girl, who in her heart love abounds
For me, our dog Sasha and dancing and musical sounds
I want to cherish the moment when I stand
Next to family and friends, just as we planned
And I shake hands, give hugs and perhaps a kiss
I want to show them love during moments like this
I want moments experiencing a beach walk at sunset
I want to enjoy a big old barbecue, and I bet
I could love a moment of just relaxing a bit
Maybe in a quiet forest or even when on the recliner, I sit
Now, as I reflect on these moments during which I've written
I find I want to write poems, I guess I am smitten
By using some moments to challenge my mind
And offer you a poem to read, if you would be so kind.

Lighten Up

And now for something lighter
A full-blown blues fighter
Something a lot happier
Much more back-slappier
Think of having some good fortune
And whistle a merry tune
Okay, maybe the world is closing in
It's almost impossible to grin
May this writer something start
I'm throwing you a love dart straight from my heart.

Hold Your Ground

Wrestling with mistakes
Don't pull up stakes
Hold your ground
With God, you're safe and sound
When people don't tell you the truth
Tighten your belt of truth
Hold your ground
When fears fight you
Here's what to do
Hold your ground
Stand firm
As you come to terms
With your fears
Through the coming years.

A Little Help

For you little one, I'm going to whisper
I know if I speak up my voice would be crisper
But I came here to help settle you down
While your mommy and daddy begin to expound
On cute little ducklings and Cinderella's shoe
Hoping you fall asleep before they are through
Those folks also speak softly into your precious ears
As they make you feel safe or wipe away tears
I shall not steal all the credit from those loving hearts
But let's discuss it, let's take it apart
I'd like to take a *little* credit for this job of mine
To help little ones softly recline
And to aid in the closing of your tender eyes
Oh look, it appears sleep time came as a surprise
So, it's time for me to move along
For my next project, why I might whisper a song
For you see, I am the sandman
The legend-of-sleep man come to do what I can.

Through Baby Eyes

Through baby eyes, the world is close in
You see mommy and daddy looking for a grin
And things that squeak and things that rattle
To close those eyes, for sleep is an uphill battle
You are learning to sip from a sippy cup
You see hands that want to help you pull up
Everywhere you look, loving eyes are looking at you
As grandpa and grandma chuckle at your every achoo
You see mommy or daddy reading you a book
Right to you, as they look for your look
Then when your eyes get all blurry with a cold
You see the doctor, who appears quite bold
Later in the day, you see mommy singing a lullaby
In the hope, that you will fall asleep rather than cry
Now little one, it's time to rest and possibly dream
Of long cuddles and all that you've seen
Through the eyes of God, this little one
Is one of the best things ever done.

Idol-ing By

I once incorporated
Things I thought I was never fated
Money, money, money
Now, I think it funny
Yes, the money I idolized
I thought it was the grand prize
I also thought business success
Better than all the rest
Once I thought of travel
But that since unraveled
Then there was fame
I would never stay the same
Money?
Forget about it, honey
It is fine
But I am inclined
To define
This life of mine
As not needing a dime
Just a little more time
To love you all
Yes, I hear the call
I look not to travel or fame
I claim
My Lord and Savior
As the ruler of my behavior
And He sings low
With my soul in tow.

Seeing Through the Night

Sleep is not often a leap
But a gentle relaxing from your head to your feet
It comes in all shapes and sizes
From one-hour naps to lengths for which they give prizes
As for shapes, I'm looking for meaning
Oh well, right now, there's nothing I'm gleaning
Let us move on to the mind's little scheme
Of course, I'm sneaking into talk of the dream
During your sleep, the noggin sets the tone
As a short feature or a full-length movie gets shone
Dreams can, at waking, disappear
Or they can make clarity appear
Sometimes you don't want them to end
Other times from monsters you must defend
It's time to end this story of the snooze
I hope I won't keep you awake, but you may choose
To sleep perchance to keep on dreaming
While your mind keeps on scheming
To surprise little-old you
With double features the whole night through

Mirror, mirror

Looking into a fresh-cleaned mirror
I squint to see myself a little clearer
In some ways, it is a rough reflection
As my eyes seek at least some perfection
Nope, my judging self begins to find
Imperfections of every kind
Silver hair barely clings atop aging scalp-skin
But I like the color even though it is thin
Then there is that face that is decades old
Full of maturing that makes me look cold
Oh, I could drone on about my mirror observations
But I will focus on God's gentle persuasions
He says I will not forever see what is in that mirror
One day my new face will shine smooth and be far
superior
So, I look back at this face and believe
In miracles of which I cannot conceive.

Joe the Cat

Joe, our man-cat, is unstoppable
I hear you doubters say that is improbable
Why I say he could become a cat in a hat
If in the hat he sat, and that is that
I know here I'm breaking the rule
Against writing a Dr. Seuss-style line, I'm a fool
No greater tragedies ever happened to delightful rhyme
Other than this little account of that cat of mine
My wife reminds me we have joint custody of this wily tike
We never know when his wiliness will strike
After we first brought him home, in the house, he disappeared
We looked all over, and it seemed weird
Flashlight in hand, I checked even the most unlikely spaces
Of him, there were absolutely no traces
But flashlight light fell on the thinking yellow eyes behind the washer
We thought and thought about how to free him without it feeling like torture
It took a broom to soft-sweep the brilliant guy out
After that little event, we started learning what he was all about
Over the years, he's done many and plenty of incredible tricks
With his neighborhood sweeps and lounging and getting his kicks
My apologies to the many fans of Dr. Seuss as I come to a close
His cat is the greatest, but Joe, by golly, purrs in impeccable prose.

Catching a Moment

A single point
I want to anoint
A moment beyond time
That is quite sublime
Catch it if you can
It's never bland
It brightens
It enlightens
It never frightens
Know that now
One sees how
To find and catch
This moment with no match
Getting still is the way
For that moment to stay
Locked in your conscious being
As worlds evolve for the seeing
Let joy and love show forth
In this caught moment of worth.

Samba in the Dark

Daylight dips into night
But I don't lose sight
As we samba in the dark
On the grass dancefloor in the park
Floating heels and toes
Fast, then it slows
For true romance and a moonlit glance
The wind keeps the beat
As the night begins to heat
Two dancers then stand
Hand-in-hand
And kiss
Just like this
My darling dancer
You gave your answer
Done sambaing in the park
Yet the fading rhythm continues to spark
Fresh memories of our samba in the dark.

When Kindness Comes

The earth becomes
A joyous place
Where time and space
Are racing
Toward replacing
Heartaches of life
 And burn the trials and strife
To rise from the ashes
As the burden passes
So, when kindness days come
This world will become
A place of love and laughter
This day may arrive after
Satan's day is in the past
And kindness comes home at last
Of course, we can spread kindness now
I think we all know just how.

Changing Direction

Right now, I am thinking
My mind-eye is blinking
As those who spout doubt
Seem more in than out
As far as I am concerned
That is what I learned
Despite this, I say, let there be light
As my optimism takes flight
Arise many obstacles
Possibly even in multiple
I'm riding an ocean current now
Bolstered by winds questioning how
We cannot rise
To heights among the skies
So, let us hope again
As to the world, I send
A word of healing
And of love revealing.

When a Door Opens

When a door closes
One supposes
Life has taken a topsy-turvy turn
And you won't ever return
To a straight path ahead
But God has other plans instead
And opens another door
Entering, you can explore
New ways to live
And to give
Back to the one
God's only son.

Looking Long

I am looking long
As I go along
Past hopefully unenduring things
Like past hurts and stings
At least, that's what I say
Let those burdens float away
As God takes me in his arms
And shields me from all alarms
Yes, I am looking long
With God's help, I'll stay strong.

Renewal

God brings renewal
It's His fuel
For setting things right
Sometimes changing overnight
Our pathway to light
That is shining bright
Showing solid insight
I pray for renewal now
Of my wedding vow
Of my life's purpose
Of my need for a surplus
Of beautiful deeds
That creates the seeds
Of things eternal
If even just a kernel.

My Soul

It is fine
But I am inclined
To define
This life of mine
As not needing a dime
Just a little more time
To love you all
Yes, I hear the call
I look not to travel or fame
I claim
My Lord and Savior
As the ruler of my behavior
And He sings low
With my soul in tow

And Now It's 2020

(January thoughts)
Rung in it is
2020 is here
A decade done
Now on to the '20s
The year has just begun
I want to take a moment
To look ahead
To a wonderful winter
A super spring
A fantastic fall
And a presidential election
May all turn out well
For each individual
As time marches
From season to season
My New Year's resolution
Is for a year full of joy
And laughter
I pray these things
In Jesus's name
HAPPY NEW YEAR!

What to Say

There comes a day
When you wonder what to say
I'm not wondering anymore
I know for sure
I say settle in
And begin more to depend
On our most high God and friend
I say let's follow the CDC's lead
And never impede
And with all-speed
Say a cluster of prayers
To the Man Upstairs
I say soon will come a day
When we pack all the fear away.

God and the Pandemic

(The early days)
Looking for you, God
Looking for your strength
Looking for your guidance
Looking for your wisdom
Looking for love when we cannot cuddle
Looking for comfort when we cannot huddle
Looking for companions in empty streets
Looking for toilet paper and hand sanitizers
Looking for hope from the media, from the government
Looking for a lift from the clergy
We are at the early stages just now
And most don't even know just how
To forecast an end
But wait a minute, dear friend
God is not hiding
He is presiding
He doesn't need to social distance
No, he holds our hand
And dries our tears
He's hurting too
But remains the glue
That keeps our souls safe
And helps us take
Great leaps of faith
That brings about the touch
That heals us so much

At Home

At home, at home, at home
Not allowed to roam
Except to a grocery store
Where toilet paper is no more
Or to the pharmacy for drugs
In case we harbor some cootie bugs
At home, we learn
With lots of time to burn
By reading a book
Or taking a look
At our laundry pile
But decide to wile
Away the time with a newspaper
Or raiding the refrigerator
Then decide to linger
After dinner
On the comfortable recliner
For we cannot go to the diner
So, we check out the TV news
And take a snooze
How about writing a poem
That you could show them?
The best thing about these days
Is that we can stay all day in our PJs
Don't forget to wash and wash and wash your hands
With super soaps of any brands.

Impatience Burn

Patience in particular

On foot or vehicular

Comes slowly to me

It is about my mind, you see

We do not always agree

Sometimes it creates a rush

Yes, even a push

For a quick resolution

To the exclusion

Of a measured pace

More toward an unreal space

Where things get done

As if I am the only one

Surely, one day I will learn

To stop the impatience burn

And douse that fire

May it inspire

Me to seldom

Create such mental bedlam

Which agitate

My mindful state

Let my impatience blaze

Be doused as patience I raise

To the front of my mind

Yes, leave impatience behind.

Lighten Up

And now for something lighter
A full-blown blues fighter
Something a lot happier
Much more back-slappier
Think of having some good fortune
And whistle a merry tune
Okay, maybe the world is closing in
It's almost impossible to grin
May this writer something start
I'm throwing you a love dart straight from my heart.

Acknowledgments

Many friends, family, and coworkers, perhaps unknowingly, helped me form this memoir, but I want to expressly thank a couple of folks who contributed heavily to birthing this tome.

Alphabetically, I salute Russell Autrey, whose artwork graces the cover. I attended high school with him some 50 years ago in Bryan, Texas. He visited me while I was on Highway 21. He since blossomed into a successful photographer, author, and artist.

Retired to a beach home in Port Bolivar, Texas, Russell continues taking fantastic photographs, now mainly of shorebirds near his home. One of his premier works is the book The Bolivar Point Lighthouse. It features his spectacular photos of the historic lighthouse in need of refurbishing. An accompanying story of the lighthouse is by Denise Adams.

I am also indebted to Ernie Lee for editing the memoir and publishing it. Ernie was in the same high school in Bryan as Russell and me back in the 1960s. He and his family took several vacations together over the years.

Ernie went on to successful careers in several areas. He is a noted author of several novels, including Cosplay, The Comic-Con Killer."

Ernie heads Aim-Hi Publishing, which he created some years ago.